# HOW TO AVOID A
# TAX AUDIT
# OF YOUR RETURN

## THE
## J. K. LASSER TAX INSTITUTE

### Editor, Bernard Greisman

SIMON AND SCHUSTER | NEW YORK

HOW TO AVOID A TAX AUDIT OF YOUR RETURN

Published by Simon and Schuster, Inc.
Simon and Schuster Building
Rockefeller Center
1230 Avenue of the Americas
New York, New York 10020
SIMON AND SCHUSTER and colophon are registered
trademarks of Simon & Schuster, Inc.

Designed by Irving Perkins Associates
Manufactured in the United States of America

1 2 3 4 5 6 7 8 9 10

ISBN: 0-671-52922-6

# CONTENTS

**PREFACE**

**PART ONE**

**6 Contents**

## PART TWO

## 8 Contents

# PREFACE

Nearly two million tax returns will be examined this year. Since over ninety million returns are filed annually, you may consider the odds of your being audited just a cold statistic. But if the odds do not hold up in your case, and your return is picked for IRS review, you will suddenly come face-to-face with the reality of having to defend your return. This book will guide you through the IRS examination and appeal procedures, pointing out your rights, choices of action, and strategies.

Even if you are lucky—your return is not picked by the IRS for audit—you should be familiar with the way the IRS selects and audits returns. You will find that this knowledge will broaden your perspective in making tax decisions and in preparing a return which will pass an IRS review.

Part One of this book presents a step-by-step guide to examinations and appeals so that you know what to expect and how to plan for your defense. Also included is a chapter explaining the general structure of the federal income tax law so that, if you must argue a point of tax law, you may be able to distinguish the various legal authorities that support your position.

Part Two of the book presents a substantial excerpt from an audit guide handbook prepared by the Internal Revenue Service for Agents examining individual tax returns. The guide will give you the perspective of an examination from an Agent's point of view and help you prepare your case more thoroughly by allowing you to anticipate the auditor's position.

We gratefully acknowledge the contribution of Elliott Eiss, member of the New York Bar, and the assistance of Katherine Torak, in the preparation of this book.

Bernard Greisman,
Editor, J. K. Lasser Tax Institute

# HOW TO AVOID A TAX AUDIT OF YOUR RETURN

# PART ONE

# —1—

# How to Avoid Tax Examinations

The odds are low that your return will be picked for audit. The IRS does not have the personnel and resources to examine every return so it selects those returns which upon preliminary inspection have a high audit potential—those that are most likely to result in a substantial tax deficiency. In recent years, less than 2% of all individual income tax returns have been examined, and the number has been decreasing, from about 2% of all 1979 returns to about 1.55% of individual returns in 1981. These low figures may seem reassuring but can also be misleading. For high income individuals, the audit percentage is substantially greater. If you claim tax shelter writeoffs, the odds of being audited increase sharply. What you must do is avoid the trouble spots that may trigger IRS suspicion. Careful preparation of your return can reduce the odds of it being selected for audit, and, if you are audited, improves your chances of defending the return.

Prior dealings with the IRS or information obtained by the IRS from third parties may increase the chances of your being audited, as in the following circumstances:

1. A prior audit resulted in a tax deficiency.
2. You requested a ruling or determination letter on a particular issue or transaction.
3. An informer gives the IRS grounds to believe that you are omitting income from your return.
4. You make an unusually large bank deposit. Banks are required to report deposits of more than $10,000 to the IRS.
5. Your state tax return has been audited. A state may report changes to the IRS after a state audit.
6. The Social Security Administration contacts the IRS under the belief that you did not report all your income when filing for benefits.
7. You are a doctor who has received a payment of $25,000 under Medicare or Medicaid.

## How the IRS Picks Returns for Audit

Returns are rated for audit by a computer formula called the discriminant factor system or DIF. To rank returns according to their audit potential, items on the return are weighted on the basis of data compiled from extensive audits of taxpayers under the Taxpayer Compliance Measurement Program (TCMP). Since its inception in 1969, the DIF method has aided the IRS in selecting returns subject to tax deficiencies. Although the details of the DIF formula are not made public, it is known that the formula considers the amount and type of income reported. Individual returns are grouped according to the total of all income items reported on the return without regard to losses. The total is called total positive income or TPI. Business returns are grouped according to total gross receipts or TGR.

The following chart, based on IRS annual reports, gives a general idea of the likelihood that a return will be audited.

The chart compares the audit percentage for returns filed in 1981 with those filed in 1982.

| Individuals' nonbusiness TPI of between | Audit percentage | |
|---|---|---|
| | 1981 returns | 1982 returns |
| $10,000 to $25,000 with itemized deductions | 2.45% | 2.15% |
| $10,000 to $25,000 without itemized deductions | .57% | .64% |
| $25,000 to $50,000 | 2.90% | 2.61% |
| Over $50,000 | 5.68% | 4.93% |
| Professional or business income on Schedule C of | | |
| $25,000 to $100,000 | 3.97% | 3.28% |
| $100,000 or over | 5.94% | 6.12% |
| Partnerships | 1.63% | 2.41% |

The chances of your being audited may also depend on where you live. Audit rates are higher in cities with a concentration of high earners. The chart below indicates that

## AUDIT PERCENTAGE

| | Individual Returns | | Partnerships | |
|---|---|---|---|---|
| | 1982 | 1981 | 1982 | 1981 |
| Manhattan, N.Y. | 2.51% | 2.21% | 5.98% | 1.78% |
| Chicago, Ill. | 1.27% | 1.44% | 2.50% | 1.52% |
| San Francisco, Cal. | 1.84% | 1.87% | 2.00% | 1.44% |
| Atlanta, Ga. | 1.37% | 1.50% | 2.04% | 1.69% |
| Boston, Mass. | 0.88% | 1.12% | 3.45% | 2.11% |
| Dallas, Tex. | 1.37% | 1.33% | 2.21% | 1.06% |

audit rates are higher for individuals in San Francisco or Chicago than in Boston, but the audit rate for partnerships is higher in Boston. Note that the IRS has intensified its audits of partnerships; the audit rate for 1982 partnerships was significantly higher than for 1981 returns in all localities, especially in Manhattan.

Your return may command special IRS scrutiny because of your profession, type of transactions reported, or deductions claimed. The chances of being audited are greater under these circumstances:

1. You claim tax shelter losses.
2. You report complex investment or business transactions without clear explanations.
3. You receive cash payments in your work which the IRS thinks are easy to conceal, such as cash fees received by doctors or tips received by cab drivers and waiters.
4. Business expenses are large in relation to income.
5. Cash contributions to charity are large in relation to income.
6. You use head of household rates to figure your tax, without noting the name of the qualifying dependent. This attracts IRS attention and results in a form letter requesting additional information.
7. You are a shareholder of a close corporation whose return has been examined.


## Tax Shelter Investors Are Targeted for Audit

The odds of your being audited increase when you claim tax shelter losses. For example, about 325,000 returns with tax shelter items were under IRS examination as of October 1983; of these, 78,000 audits were completed during 1983 and deductions were disallowed in 93% of the cases. On average, investors were assessed an extra $18,000 in tax and penalties.

The IRS has also adopted what it calls a "front-end" attack against "abusive" tax shelter schemes. The IRS strategy involves setting up teams of auditors and attorneys to look into tax shelter promotions as soon as they go public.

What is an "abusive" shelter? There is no precise definition, but the IRS is suspicious of any promotion offering tax writeoffs which are far in excess of the cash investment and loans for which investors are personally liable.

The IRS may examine the promoter's financial books and investor records if it suspects that the promised writeoffs violate the tax law. Penalties may be assessed against the promoter, and the IRS can even go to court to stop promotion of the shelter.

If you have invested in a shelter which the IRS determines is abusive, it may send you a letter warning that certain deductions will be disallowed, that your return will be audited, and that you may be assessed penalties in addition to the extra tax. The goal of the IRS is to send these warnings before you file your return in order to deter you from claiming the writeoffs. If you receive the letter after you file your return and do not file an amended return without the deduction, you will be audited.

Tax shelters generally have to register with the IRS and receive an identification number which an investor must include in his or her tax return. Audits of tax shelter partnerships are generally conducted at the partnership level.

The message is clear: Investigate before you invest in a tax shelter. Consult with a tax adviser about potential tax disputes with the IRS. Do not rely on the tax opinion included in the prospectus, which might underplay potential problems. If possible, check the promoter's past record.

## A Refund Claim May Lead to an Audit

A refund claim may trigger an audit. The threshold amount at which a refund claim is examined depends on the particular IRS office involved and its work load.

Before filing for a refund of taxes, carefully review all of the items on your return. The item on which you base the refund claim may be sound, but other items on your return may be questionable. If the amount of tax involved in these other items equals or exceeds your refund claim, it may be unwise to file a claim and open your return to an audit. Refund claims based on overwithholding of taxes will not lead to an audit.

## Deductions Which the IRS Questions

Casualty and theft loss deductions. These deductions, the amounts of which are often open to estimate, are trouble spots. Take the case of storm damage to your home: The amount of loss is usually measured by the drop in market value caused by the casualty, but two appraisers can come up with different amounts. The IRS is aware of this leeway and will generally scrutinize deductions taken for large casualty losses. A fully documented explanation of the background of your loss and the basis for your calculation may satisfy the IRS examiner. If you claim a theft loss deduction, give the background and details of the theft, and also the date on which you reported the theft to the police.

Charitable contributions. Claiming a large amount of cash donations may trigger an IRS check. In 1982, the IRS began to review approximately 30,000 returns which reported deductions for cash contributions exceeding 35%

of adjusted gross income. If questioned, you must prove your donation by either a canceled check or a receipt from the organization showing the date of contribution, the amount, and the name of the donee. If there is no canceled check or receipt, the IRS may accept other written evidence showing the name of the donee, and the amount and date of the contribution. For instance, a diary entry made on the date of the expenditure may be considered reliable depending on the facts and circumstances of your particular case. Even without any written evidence, local IRS offices have guidelines which allow a certain amount to be deducted; the amount varies, depending on your income and where you live.

If you claim property donations, a large deduction for donations of second-hand merchandise will catch the reviewer's eye. To support these deductions, the IRS requires that statements be submitted with your return. If you donate property, such as paintings, furniture, clothing, realty, or securities, you should attach a statement describing the property, the date of the gift, and for all property other than securities, how you valued it. If the value of the gift exceeds $200, and for gifts of capital gain or ordinary income property, state whether or not there are any conditions attached to the gift, how you acquired the property, and the cost or other basis of the property if it was owned by you for less than five years, and submit a signed copy of an appraisal, if you have one. You must have an appraisal for a donation after 1984 of property other than publicly-traded stock, if it exceeds $5,000 ($10,000 for non-publicly traded stock); a summary of the appraisal is attached to your return. You must also attach a schedule explaining the computation of a deduction for depreciable property, or for personal property, such as art objects, which will not be used by the charity for its exempt purposes.

Increase in exemptions. If your return shows an increase in the number of exemptions which is unusual for your family status, the computer may pick your return for review. An exemption claim for someone other than a child may also be questioned.

Bad debt deduction. Deductions for bad debts are a prime suspect area for IRS scrutiny. If you claim a bad debt, be sure you deduct it as a short-term capital loss unless you have sound grounds to show that the debt was incurred in your business.

The IRS requires that you attach a statement giving the details: The nature of the bad debt; name of the debtor and his relationship to you, if any; when the debt was due; how you tried to collect it; why you decided it was worthless this year. Evidence of the debtor's insolvency is usually satisfactory proof of worthlessness. If the loan was made to a relative, the IRS will presume it to be a gift. You need strong evidence to support your claim that you made a bona fide loan, and not a gift. You should show that interest was charged and attempts made to collect the debt, in addition to evidence that it became worthless.

Home office deduction. Claiming a deduction for home office expenses may invite IRS scrutiny. The deduction is subject to severe limitations. In order to deduct the expenses allocable to the office, the office must be used exclusively on a regular basis as your principal place of business, or as a place of business used by patients, clients, or customers in meeting with you in the normal course of your business. If you are an employee, the office must be used for your employer's convenience. The office must be used solely for your business or job; it may not also be used for personal purposes or for a combination of personal and business purposes. The deduction may not exceed the gross income derived from your office. Because of these limitations, the IRS questions the validity of many home-office deductions. Claiming the deduction may put you in a higher audit classification under the DIF system, but, if you qualify, take the deduction and attach a statement explaining how you meet the legal requirements. The statement may help avoid an audit on the home-office issue.

Travel and entertainment expenses. Large amounts of travel expenses are a prime target of IRS reviewers. Basic to supporting your deduction is filing a statement explaining the deduction; failure to do so may lead to an automatic review of your return. If you use your car for business travel, failure to show some allocation to personal driving may prompt a review. You must use a car placed in service after June 18, 1984 more than 50% of the time for business to claim ACRS depreciation or an investment credit. Further, after 1984 you must keep a log showing the dates of business trips and mileage driven.

Restrictive tests apply to deductions taken for entertainment on yachts, and at country clubs, sports arenas, theaters, and other nonbusiness settings. These may be prime targets for an audit.

Deducting job expenses in the wrong place. Wage earners who incur entertainment expenses or expenses for union dues and work clothes must deduct these only as excess itemized deductions. If you do not claim excess itemized deductions because itemized deductions do not exceed your zero bracket amount (formerly the standard deduction), claiming these expenses as deductions under the heading "adjustments to income" on Form 1040 will trigger an audit.

## Are There Guidelines for Estimating Deductions?

The IRS has published a guideline only for deducting sales and gasoline taxes. The IRS does have standards for various tax brackets which are figured into the DIF formula for grading returns for audit, but these are secret. However, the IRS does release statistics showing the average deductions claimed by taxpayers according to adjusted gross income groups. The table below, based on these statistics, indicates the average amounts deducted by individuals on their 1982 individual returns. These figures, the latest available, are presented only for comparison with your own deductions. You are not entitled to claim the average deduction without substantiation; if audited, you must prove your deductions. Clearly, however, it is more likely that your return will be flagged for audit if your deductions are substantially larger than the average for your income group.

| Adjusted gross income (thousands) | Interest | Medical Expenses | Taxes | Donations |
|---|---|---|---|---|
| $ 12–16 | $ 2,454 | $1,247 | $ 1,261 | $ 754 |
| 16–20 | 2,564 | 893 | 1,471 | 666 |
| 20–30 | 3,082 | 830 | 1,944 | 727 |
| 30–40 | 3,596 | 690 | 2,575 | 860 |
| 40–50 | 4,482 | 843 | 3,237 | 1,148 |
| 50–75 | 6,240 | 900 | 4,575 | 1,550 |
| 75–100 | 8,720 | 1,028 | 6,920 | 2,525 |
| 100–200 | 13,900 | 1,560 | 10,200 | 4,650 |

## Failure to Report Income as Listed on Information Returns

If you want to avoid having your return questioned, correctly report income, no matter how small, which is documented by withholding or other information returns. Attach to your return Form W-2 reporting wage income and list your Social Security number. When your return is received by the IRS Service Center, the amount of salary or wages reported on your return is matched by computer with the Form W-2 filed by your employer.

The IRS has not been as successful in matching tax returns with other types of information returns, such as Form 1099 for reporting interest and dividends. Forms 1099 are sent to the IRS by payers on paper forms, rather than on magnetic tape; though virtually all information returns reported on magnetic tape are matched against information returns, the IRS has lacked the manpower to process the paper forms. The IRS has been encouraging the use of magnetic tape, which, in the future, should result in closer matching of amounts reported by individuals with the Forms 1099 reported by payers.

If the IRS finds a discrepancy between the income you report and the amount reported on Form 1099, such as if you fail to report interest from a bank account or a Treasury Bill, it will send you a letter pointing out the error and recomputing your tax, with interest if due. The letter will spell out your appeal rights in case you disagree with the determination. If the IRS detects a pattern of omitting income, it may select the return for audit.

To avoid questioning of your return, be sure you receive statements from all banks, mutual funds, corporations and other payers of income to you and report the correct amount to the IRS.

Underreporting of interest and dividend income can also result in the imposition of 20% "backup" withholding by the IRS. "Backup" withholding is required only if income has been underreported, or if you fail to provide the correct Social Security number to banks or other payers.

The IRS also monitors your reporting of gains and losses from sales of stocks and other securities. Brokers report to the IRS on Form 1099-B your sales of stocks, bonds, commodities, futures contracts and forward contracts. You receive a copy of Form 1099-B but it does not have to be attached to your return.

Exchanges of property or services through a broker are also reported to the IRS on Form 1099-B. The IRS has been cracking down on barter exchanges which it considers to be a growing source of tax avoidance.

State and local tax refunds of $10 or more, including credits and offsets, are also reported to the IRS on Form 1099-G, a copy of which you receive. The IRS is interested in state and local tax refunds because if you claimed the taxes as an itemized deduction on your federal return, part or all of the refund is generally taxable in the year you receive it.

Restaurant and bar owners with more than 10 employees have to allocate a certain amount of tip income to their employees and file this information with the IRS on Form 941. The excess of 8% of the owner's gross receipts over the amount of tips actually reported by the employees to the owner must be allocated for employees who receive tips. If the employer or majority of employees shows that the average tip rate is below 8%, the allocation rate may be reduced to as low as 2%. If you receive tips, your Form W-2 notes the amount of tip income allocated to you by your employer. Because the new rules assume that employees receive tip income of at least 8%, employees who report lower tip income may be targeted for audit. If audited, you must be able to produce records showing that you received tips below 8%. The IRS could rule that you should have reported larger tips than those required under the 8% allocation rule where the establishment's credit charge receipts indicate a tip rate of more than 8%.

## If You Are Picked for a TCMP Audit

Regardless of how careful you are in preparing your return, you may not be able to avoid an audit conducted by the IRS under its Taxpayer Compliance Measurement Program, or TCMP. About every two years, taxpayers are randomly selected for TCMP audits.

A TCMP is much more extensive than a regular audit. In effect, you are being used for research. The IRS selects you as a representative of your income class; extremely detailed audits are necessary because they provide the raw data for developing the DIF formulas which rate returns according to their audit potential.

Because of the research value of TCMP, IRS agents will check *every line* on your return. Nothing is taken for granted. A deduction will not be allowed because it seems "reasonable." The examining Agent will, at the least, ask you about every item and may ask you to provide documentary proof. For example, if you file a joint return, you may be asked to show your marriage license. A birth certificate may have to be shown to substantiate a dependency exemption for your child.

The only bright side to TCMP is that the odds of your being selected are extremely low; only about one in two thousand. Approximately 50,000 individual returns for 1982 were selected by the IRS for TCMP audit.

## Running the Risk of an Audit

The previous pages covered areas vulnerable to audit and possible ways to avoid them. Sometimes, you may not be able to avoid them, and sound tax planning may even require running a risk of tax examination. Not all answers to tax transactions are clear-cut. There is room for estimates and for honest differences of opinion. That the IRS may disagree with a particular position you take on your tax return should not discourage you from taking the position if it is sound and reasonable. You may eventually win your point. If you should lose, the cost is the tax you would have paid anyway, plus interest. The interest rate is subject to change every six months. An 11% rate, compounded daily, applies to the period between July 1, 1983 and December 31, 1984.

# 2

# How to Prepare for the Examination

A notice from the IRS that your return is being questioned will usually arouse anxiety. You may have an exaggerated fear that some misstatement on your return *will* lead to a fraud charge, or that your personal life and finances are now open to a bureaucratic inquisition. Before causing yourself unnecessary worry, check to see exactly what the IRS is questioning. It may concern a single item, such as interest income, which you should have reported but did not or a deduction you claimed which the IRS thinks is improper. These types of problems may even be solved without a face-to-face meeting with an IRS examiner.

## The IRS Handles Many Problems By Mail

When the IRS receives your return, computers check it for mathematical errors. If you underpaid your tax, the IRS will send you a form letter showing the mistake and billing you for the additional tax, plus interest. If you paid too much tax, you should receive a refund.

Your return will also be spot-checked for items exceeding the limits specified by law. This "unallowable items" program is handled through correspondence and eliminates the need for an audit interview. These types of errors are handled by mail:

Deducting auto mileage rates for business transportation in excess of 20.5¢ per mile for the first 15,000 miles or 11¢ per mile over 15,000 miles;

Claiming dividend exclusions in excess of $100 or $200 on a joint return;

Claiming a fractional exemption for a person whom you help support;

Deducting personal auto license, registration and tag fees, which are nondeductible except in a small number of states;

Omitting income or claiming a deduction or credit as a protest against war or the tax system; protestors who refuse to pay an IRS deficiency are subject to additional penalties.

You are advised by mail of the corrections and additional tax due. You may avoid additional interest charges by paying the deficiency promptly.

Where an underpayment of tax results from a mathematical or clerical error, you do not have a right to appeal to the Tax Court as provided in other cases. The IRS must give you an explanation of the error and 60 days in which to file a request for abatement of the assessment. The IRS must honor that request and follow the normal deficiency procedure. This procedure applies to the following types of mathematical and clerical errors: (1) arithmetic errors (addition, subtraction, multiplication, or division); (2) errors in transferring amounts on the tax forms; (3) missing schedules or forms; (4) incorrect use of a Treasury table; and (5) entries that exceed statutory limitations.

Where an arithmetical error is made by an IRS taxpayer service representative, the Treasury may abate any interest due on the underpayment of tax for any period ending on or before the 30th day following the date of notice and demand for payment of the deficiency. Contact the Penalty Abatement Officer in your district to eliminate improper interest charges. In all other cases, interest is payable on a deficiency and runs from the date the return is due until the underpayment is paid.

DIF—selected returns may be handled by mail.   The fact that the IRS computer gives your return a high audit-potential score does not mean it will be selected for audit by an Agent. The IRS may send you a letter asking for additional information about the queried items. For example, if you have claimed an exceptionally high medical expense deduction, the IRS will mail you a specific questionnaire for documenting the deduction. Similarly, the IRS has questionnaires for charitable contributions, taxes, interest and job expenses. Answer the questionnaire and attach to it copies of receipts and canceled checks that substantiate the claimed expenses.

If the IRS is not satisfied with your answers to a questionnaire, you may be called in for an office audit. However, if you receive a questionnaire and feel that it places you at a disadvantage, you may request an office audit if you believe you will be better able to settle the case in your favor by appearing personally.

## Types of Audits

An examination may be held at a local IRS office or at your place of business or home. An examination at an IRS office is called a desk or office examination; an examination at your place of business or home is called a field examination. The complexity of the transactions reported on your return will determine whether your return receives an office or field examination.

Department of the Treasury — Internal Revenue Service

| Form **4746**<br>(Rev. Aug. 1982) | **Questionnaire — Credit for Child and Dependent Care Expenses**<br>For Privacy Act and Paperwork Reduction Act Notice, see enclosed Notice 609. |
|---|---|

| Taxpayers' Names and Address | In Reply Refer To: |
|---|---|
| | Tax Year |

Please furnish the following information to support the child and dependent care credit on your Federal income tax return for the above year. If you need more space, please attach extra sheets. Also attach supporting documents such as receipts and canceled checks. (Photocopies are acceptable.) We will return the documents as soon as we are through with them. Thank you for your cooperation.

1. Were any of the persons for whom the payments were made physically or mentally unable to care for themselves? If so, please list by name.

A.

B.

C.

2. Please indicate the place the dependent care services were performed (for example, your home, day care center):

| | Did you file Form 942, Employer's Quarterly Tax Return for Household Employees? | |
|---|---|---|
| | Yes | No |
| A. | | |
| B. | | |
| C. | | |

3(a)  Indicate your marital status on the last day of the year in question:

Single ☐        Married ☐        Married but not living with spouse ☐

Separated under a court decree ☐     Divorced ☐     Widow ☐     Widower ☐

(b)  Please give the dates of any changes in your marital status during the tax year in question. Show also your income and your total dependent care expenses for each period.

| Date of Change in status | Income prior to change | Dependent Care Expenses prior to change |
|---|---|---|
| | | |

(over)

Form **4746** (Rev. 8

| Joint return filers use column A for wife and column B for husband. All other individuals use column C. | Joint Return | | |
|---|---|---|---|
| | A (Wife) | B (Husband) | C (Others) |
| 4(a)  Were you either working or looking for work on all days for which you paid child and dependent care expenses? (Answer Yes or No.) | | | |
| (b)  If you answered No to 4(a), what was the total amount of payments for days when you were neither working nor looking for work? | | | |
| 5(a)  Did you work full time? (Answer Yes or No.) | | | |
| (b)  If you worked part time, how many hours a day did you work? <br><br> (c)  How many days a week did you work? | | | |

Explanation of item 1:

A qualifying person is one who lived in your house as a member of your family and is:

1. Your dependent under age 15 who can be claimed as an exemption; or
2. A dependent (or a person you could claim as a dependent, if it were not for the gross income test) who is physically or mentally incapable of caring for himself or herself; or
3. Your spouse, who is physically or mentally incapable of caring for himself or herself.

If you are divorced, legally separated under a decree of divorce or separate maintenance, or separated under a written separation agreement, your child or stepchild qualifies if you had custody for a longer time during the calendar year than the other parent. Your child does not have to be your dependent. Your child must also have:

1. Been under age 15, or not able to care for himself or herself, and
2. Been in the custody of one or both parents for more than half the year, and
3. Received more than half of his or her support from one or both parents.

| Declaration <br> I declare that I have examined the information on this form and, to the best of my knowledge and belief, it is true, correct, and complete. | Your Signature | Date |
|---|---|---|
| | Spouse's Signature (if a joint return was filed) | Date |

Form **4746** (Rev. 8/82)

| Form **4748**<br>(Rev. Nov. 1982) | Department of the Treasury — Internal Revenue Service<br>**Questionnaire-Casualty or Theft Loss** | OMB No. 1545-0403<br>Expires 7/31/85) |
|---|---|---|

| Taxpayer's name and address | In reply refer to |
|---|---|
| | Tax year |

Please furnish the following information to support the deduction for casualty or theft loss shown on your Federal income tax return for the above tax year. If you had more than one loss or need more space, please use the back of this form and number the items to correspond with those below. Attach documents, such as receipts and canceled checks, to substantiate the loss and the amount. *(Photocopies are acceptable.)* We will return the documents as soon as we are through with them. Thank you for your cooperation.

1. Describe property *(If automobile, show year, make, and body style)*

| 2. Were you the legal owner of the property?<br><br>☐ Yes ☐ No | 3. On what date did you acquire the property? | 4. How long was the property in your possession? | 5. What was the cost? (Or other basis of determining value?) | 6. On what date did the loss occur? |
|---|---|---|---|---|

7. Describe nature of loss

8. Has any portion of the property been recovered?          ☐ Yes          ☐ No

9. Did you notify the police?     ☐ Yes     ☐ No     *(If Yes, please furnish a copy of the police report)*

10. Show fair market value of the property at time of loss and explain how you determined this value.

11. Show fair market value of the property immediately after loss and explain how you determined this value.

12. Was the property insured?     ☐ Yes     ☐ No<br>If Yes, please show—

| a. Name and address of insurance company | b. Maximum amount of coverage<br><br>$ | c. Amount of insurance compensation received<br>$ |
|---|---|---|

*(Please furnish a copy of the insurance settlement report.)*

13. What amount have you spent to replace, repair, or restore the property?  $
   *(This amount should not include any expenditures for improving or expanding the property beyond its original condition.)*

14. a. Has legal action been taken to recover any of the loss?     ☐ Yes     ☐ No<br>   b. If Yes, please show any amount you recovered or expect to recover  $

| **DECLARATION**<br><br>I declare that I have examined this statement and, to the best of my knowledge and belief, it is true, correct, and complete. | Your Signature | Date |
|---|---|---|
| | Spouse's Signature If a Joint Return Was Filed | Date |

For Privacy Act and Paperwork Reduction Act Notice, see back of form.          Form **4748** (Rev. 11/82)

| orm **4752**<br>Rev. October 1983) | Department of the Treasury — Internal Revenue Service<br>## Questionnaire—Head of Household | |
|---|---|---|
| axpayer's Name and Address | In Reply Refer To | |
| | Taxable Year | |

If you qualify as head of household, you are entitled to figure your tax by a special rate. However, you must meet certain requirements to obtain this benefit. Please furnish the information requested below so that we can determine whether you qualify for the above year. If you need more space, use the back of this orm. Thank you for your cooperation.

1. Check the box that shows your marital status at the end of the above tax year:

☐ Married          ☐ Single          ☐ Widowed *(Show date of spouse's death* _____ *)*

☐ Legally Separated *(Show date of legal separation* _____ *)* ☐ Divorced *(Show date of final decree* _____ *)*

☐ Separated, but not by legal separation or decree of divorce *(Show date of separation* _____ *or interlocutory decree* _____ *)*

2. Did you provide a home during the above tax year for any one of the following relatives? *(Check the box(es) that applies.)*

☐ Your child *(including stepchild, legally adopted child, child placed with you for adoption by an authorized placement agency, or foster child).*

☐ Your grandchild.          ☐ Other relative *(Show the relationship to you* _____ *)*

3. (a) If the person in item 2, was your child or grandchild was the person unmarried at the end of the tax year?  ☐ Yes  ☐ No

(b) If the person in item 2 was not your unmarried child or grandchild, did you claim this person as a dependent for the above tax year?  ☐ Yes  ☐ No

4. Did this person live with you in your principal home during the whole tax year shown above?  ☐ Yes  ☐ No

(a) If no, show the period of absence and give the reason for the absence. _____

_____

(b) If the person(s) in item 2 was your mother and/or father who did not live in your home, show the address where the person(s) lived and the number of months in the above year that your parent(s) lived at this address.

_____

| | | |
|---|---|---|
| (a) Show the total cost of keeping up the household where your relative lived for the year. *(Figure the costs below)* | $ | |
| (b) Of this amount, how much did you provide? | $ | |
| (c) Of this amount, how much did your relative provide for himself or herself? | $ | |
| (d) Of this amount, how much did others provide? *(Show name of person(s) or agency.)* | $ | |

### Cost of Keeping Up a Home

You are keeping up a home only if you pay more than half of the cost of its upkeep.

Include such costs as rent, mortgage interest, real estate taxes, insurance on the home, repairs, utilities, domestic help, and food eaten in the home.

**DO NOT INCLUDE** the cost of clothing, education, medical treatment, vacations, life insurance, transportation, rental value of your home, or value of your services or those of a member of your household.

Use these expenses only to figure whether you are keeping up a home. Do not claim them as deductions on your tax return unless they are otherwise deductible.

| Item | Amount | |
|---|---|---|
| Rent | $ | |
| Mortgage Interest | $ | |
| Real Estate Taxes | $ | |
| Home Insurance | $ | |
| Utilities | $ | |
| Home Repairs | $ | |
| Domestic Help | $ | |
| Food Eaten in Home | $ | |
| Total Cost | $ | |

| **DECLARATION**<br>I declare that I have examined this statement and, to the best of my knowledge and belief, it is true, correct, and complete. | Your Signature | Date |
|---|---|---|

Form 4752 (Rev. 10-83)

Most audits of individual returns, about 80%, are conducted at IRS offices. An office audit usually covers only a few specific issues which the IRS specifies in its notice to you. For example, the examining agent may only be interested in seeing proof for charitable deductions, medical expenses, or educational expenses.

When the IRS notifies you about an impending office audit, it usually gives you several weeks' notice to prepare your records and consult with a tax adviser. If you are unable to keep the appointment, contact the IRS office in advance; rescheduling is usually not a problem.

Field audits generally involve business returns; they are more extensive and time consuming than office audits and are handled by more experienced IRS agents. It is advisable to have a tax professional go over the potential weak spots in your return and represent you at the examination.

The examining Agent may schedule a field audit at your representative's office, your business premises, or even your home. If at all possible, *refuse* to have a field audit conducted in your own home.

## Should You Be Represented by a Tax Professional?

Ask yourself: Can I adequately represent myself? A layman can handle some issues without professional help; others require the advice of an attorney or experienced CPA. For example, you may be able to handle a case involving only factual issues of proof, such as the amount of your travel or charitable expenses.

Generally speaking, it pays to have professional assistance under these conditions: You face a potentially large deficiency; your return includes complicated business or investment transactions; or defense of your position depends on ambiguous or conflicting legal authorities. In estimating the cost of professional advice, remember that the fee is deductible.

You must give your attorney or CPA a power of attorney to represent you before the IRS. An accountant who is not a CPA or a non-accountant tax preparer must have passed an examination to be enrolled to practice before the IRS.

If, in the course of an audit, an IRS Special Agent is assigned to your case, consult an attorney immediately. The presence of a Special Agent is evidence that the IRS suspects you of tax fraud.

Before deciding to handle the audit yourself, consider the following:

1. Your time. If your return is fairly complicated, can you personally afford the time for an extensive examination?

2. Your ability to discuss the complications of the case. A general guide to weighing legal issues and the difficulties involved is presented in Chapter 4.

3. Your ability based on past experience, to keep a cool head and present your material ably and calmly. This is essential if you decide to go it alone. If you do not think you can remain businesslike during an audit, have a professional represent you. You can prejudice your case if, in the course of the audit, you take out your frustrations on the Agent. It does no good to complain about the tax system or the unfairness of the audit, which may only antagonize the Agent. Though you should not be hostile, avoid the opposite extreme and refrain from small talk. You must be able to respond politely to the Agent's questions without volunteering information that may give the Agent a new basis for questioning your return. You may be forced to concede where you cannot support your position, but do not confess that you knew you were wrong when you prepared the return. A confession of wrongdoing

gives the Agent a basis for imposing a penalty and might even lead to a referral to the Criminal Investigation Unit for a fraud investigation.

Are you likely to be intimidated by an aggressive agent? A representative is less likely to be, and, in his presence, the Agent may be willing to "give" a little more, resulting in better settlement terms. Finally, a representative may be in a better position to appeal to the Agent's supervisor if at the end of the audit, the Agent adopts a particularly harsh stance.

You may attend the examination even if you are being represented by a professional. One strategy is to have the representative answer the Agent's questions and explain the items on your return, while your participation is limited to answering specific questions put to you by your representative. Before the examination, your representative can coach you on the types of questions which might be directed to you during the audit.

## Preparing for the Examination

After an office audit is scheduled, the first thing to do is look over your return. Refresh your memory. Examine the items the IRS questioned in its notice of audit, and organize your records accordingly. Also check the rest of your return and gather proof for items you are unsure of. At this point, you should take a broad view of your return to anticipate problems you may encounter. Before the actual examination begins, consider possible settlement terms. Assume that the Agent will assess additional tax, but establish the range you will consider reasonable. You can always change your mind, but giving some thought beforehand to possible settlement terms will help you later when settlements are actually discussed.

When you attend the audit, take only the records related

to the items questioned in the IRS notice. Do not volunteer extra records; if the Agent sees them, it might suggest new areas for him to investigate.

If you are concerned that there may be a problem of negligence or fraud, see a qualified attorney before you come into contact with an IRS official. The attorney can put your actions in perspective and help protect your legal rights. Besides, what you tell an attorney is privileged information; he cannot divulge or be forced to divulge data you give him, so you need not be concerned that disclosures to him will jeopardize your position.

A field audit of your business return is likely to involve a comprehensive examination and requires careful preparation. Together with your tax adviser, go over your return for potential areas of weakness. For example, the Agent is likely to question deductions you have claimed for business travel. If you are an incorporated professional, the corporation's deductions for expenses of company-owned cars or planes will probably be reviewed. The Agent may suspect that a portion of these business deductions are actually nondeductible personal travel costs; be prepared to substantiate the business portion of your total mileage and operating expenses.

Make sure that the examination is scheduled far enough in advance for you to get ready. Do not let the IRS hurry you into an examination until you are prepared. In some localities, particularly rural areas, the IRS may give short notice in scheduling a field audit. An Agent may even appear at your home or place of business and try to begin the audit immediately. Resist this pressure and reschedule the meeting at your convenience.

## Restrictions on IRS Examinations of Books

The IRS may not make more than one examination of your books of accounts for any taxable period unless you request otherwise, or the IRS, after investigation, notifies you in writing that an additional inspection is necessary. However, this restriction does not bar the IRS from examining public records or bank accounts.

You may protest a second examination by refusing to give the Agent access to your books. The Treasury may then issue a summons. If you still refuse access, the IRS may seek enforcement of the summons in District Court. You then have the opportunity at a hearing in the District Court to show that a second examination is unnecessary.

The IRS tries to avoid audits of items that were examined on a prior year's return, such as home-office expenses. Thus, where your return was examined in either of the two years prior to the current examination for the same items, and that audit resulted in no change in tax liability or only a small change, the IRS will suspend the current examination upon your notifying the appointment clerk or the examiner, pending a review of its files. You can expedite the process if you have kept copies of the audit appointment letter and the audit report from the prior year.

## Handling the Examination

Office audits may conclude quickly because they usually involve only a few specific issues. In some cases, the audit may take less than an hour. The key to handling the audit is advance preparation. When you arrive at the IRS office, be prepared to produce your records quickly. Records should be organized by topic so that you do not waste time leafing through pages for a receipt or other document. Careful preparation will speed up the examination, which is to your advantage; you do not want to give the Agent time to think of additional items to question on your return. Furthermore, if you can efficiently provide proof for one or two items on the Agent's list, he may even decide to forgo review of the other items.

If the Agent decides to question an item not mentioned in the notice of audit, refuse politely but firmly to answer the questions. Tell the Agent that you must first review your records. If the Agent insists on pursuing the matter, he will have to schedule another meeting. He might decide it is not worth his time and drop the issue.

Bear in mind that the Agent has a heavy case load and is as anxious as you are to conclude the audit quickly. If you prepare for the examination carefully and present your case in a calm, businesslike manner, you may be able to bring the audit to a reasonably satisfactory conclusion, even if you have to pay some additional tax.

Follow common sense rules of courtesy during the examination. Arrive on time for the office interview. Do not antagonize the Agent. It is useless to vent your anger on the Agent because you think the tax laws are unfair. He is not responsible for the tax laws and you may prejudice your case over an item that can be compromised.

While you should avoid personality clashes, be firm in your approach. If the Agent appears to be unreasonable, you or your representative should make it clear that, if necessary, you will go all the way to court to win your point. A firm approach may strengthen your ability to obtain a favorable settlement.

If the IRS has scheduled a field audit, ask that the examination be held at your representative's office. If you have not retained professional help and the examination takes place at your business premises, do not allow the agent free reign of the area: Provide him with a comfortable work area for examining your records. If possible, the workplace should be isolated so that the Agent can concentrate on the examination without being distracted by office operations that might spark questions. Tell your employees not to answer questions about your business or engage in small talk with the Agent. As with an office audit, help speed along the field examination by having prepared your records so that requested information can be quickly produced.

## Possibility of Fraud

Your inability to produce records for a claimed deduction, an error in reporting income, or a difference of opinion on how to report an item, will not give rise to charges of fraud. The American income tax system is based on self-assessment, an important fact which implies that you have the right to so arrange your affairs in order to pay the lowest possible tax. You are not, however, allowed to evade taxes. Tax evasion involves deceit, misrepresentation, and subterfuge, all of which may subject you to fraud charges. Fines and possible prison sentences could be imposed if the IRS proves that you are guilty of fraud.

Extreme or recognizable examples of fraud can be described, but it is difficult to draw the lines separating fraud from negligence and both from just plain error. If an examining Agent concludes that you have substantially underreported your income or greatly overstated deductible expenses, his suspicion may be aroused. If you cannot provide a reasonable explanation, an examining Agent who suspects fraud may prepare a referral report for the Criminal Investigation Division which will decide whether to pursue a fraud investigation. Until Criminal Intelligence makes a decision, your audit is suspended. When an IRS Special Agent contacts you, a criminal investigation has begun. At this point, do not continue with the examination and immediately consult an attorney with experience in criminal tax cases.

If you are concerned about possible fraud charges, see

a qualified attorney before you come in contact with any IRS official.

## If You Agree With the Examiner

After the Agent completes his review of your return, he will discuss proposed changes with you or your representative.

If you agree with the Agent's proposed changes, he will ask you to sign a Form 870 which, when signed, permits an immediate assessment of a deficiency plus penalties and interest, if due. A copy of Form 870 appears below, on page 42.

Before deciding whether to sign the Form 870, consider that, by signing, you are giving up your right of appeal to both an IRS Appellate conference and the Tax Court. However, you may still file a refund suit in a Federal District Court or in the Claims Court unless you have agreed not to do so on the Form 870.

If you believe that you have done as well or better than expected regarding the proposed deficiency, you can bring the case to a close by signing the Form 870, but the Agent's supervisor must also approve the assessment.

By signing the form, you limit the amount of interest charges added to the deficiency: Interest stops running within 30 days after the date it is signed.

It is possible, although unlikely, that upon examining your return, the Agent will determine that you are due a refund. In this situation, a signed Form 870 is merely an acknowledgment of the over-assessment. You should file a protective refund claim even if you sign the Form 870 acknowledging the over-assessment. Generally, the Agent will process the refund, but if he fails to do so or the review staff puts it aside for some reason and the limitations period expires, the refund will be lost. The refund claim will protect you from such a mishap.

| Department of the Treasury — Internal Revenue Service | Date received by Internal Revenue Service |
|---|---|

**Form 870**
Rev. December 1983)

**Waiver of Restrictions on Assessment and Collection of Deficiency in Tax and Acceptance of Overassessment**

| Names and address of taxpayers (Number, street, city or town, State, ZIP code) | Social security or employer identification number |
|---|---|

### Increase in Tax and Penalties

| Tax year ended | Amount of tax | Penalty |
|---|---|---|
| | $ | $ |
| | $ | $ |
| | $ | $ |

### Decrease in Tax and Penalties

| Tax year ended | Amount of tax | Penalty |
|---|---|---|
| | $ | $ |
| | $ | $ |
| | $ | $ |

*For any remarks, see back of form)*

## Instructions

### General Information

If you consent to the assessment of the deficiencies shown in this waiver, please sign and return the form in order to limit any interest charge and expedite the adjustment to your account. Your consent will not prevent you from filing a claim for refund *(after you have paid the tax)* if you later believe you are so entitled. It will not prevent us from later determining, if necessary, that you owe additional tax; nor extend the time provided by law for either action.

We have agreements with State tax agencies under which information about Federal tax, including increases or decreases, is exchanged with the States. If this change affects the amount of your State income tax, you should file the required State form.

If you later file a claim and the Service disallows it, you may file suit for refund in a district court or in the United States Claims Court, but you may not file a petition with the United States Tax Court.

We will consider this waiver a valid claim for refund or credit of any overpayment due you resulting from any decrease in tax and penalties shown above, provided you sign and file it within the period established by law for making such a claim.

### Who Must Sign

If you filed jointly, both you and your spouse must sign. If this waiver is for a corporation, it should be signed with the corporation name, followed by the signatures and titles of the corporate officers authorized to sign. An attorney or agent may sign this waiver provided such action is specifically authorized by a power of attorney which, if not previously filed, must accompany this form.

If this waiver is signed by a person acting in a fiduciary capacity *(for example, an executor, administrator, or a trustee)* Form 56, Notice Concerning Fiduciary Relationship, should, unless previously filed, accompany this form.

### Consent to Assessment and Collection

I consent to the immediate assessment and collection of any deficiencies *(increase in tax and penalties)* and accept any overassessment *(decrease in tax and penalties)* shown above, plus any interest provided by law. I understand that by signing this waiver, I will not be able to contest these years in the United States Tax Court, unless additional deficiencies are determined for these years.

| Signatures | | Date |
|---|---|---|
| | | Date |
| | By | Title | Date |

Form **870** (Rev. 12-83)

## An Agreed Case Is Always Reviewed

Once a Form 870 is signed, the Agent prepares his report and it goes to a review group in the Examination Division. Here, it gets a complete technical review. In most cases, the report is approved.

As a general rule, the reviewer will check at least:

*Facts appearing in the Agent's report and in the return filed.* Here he may develop facts which the Agent overlooked or which did not appear important to the Agent.

*Agent's interpretation of the law and the manner in which he applies its provisions to the facts in the case.*

*Agent's judgment.* You might not be able to substantiate all claimed expense deductions by primary evidence such as cancelled checks and bills. So the Agent might decide what portion of the claimed deduction (not supported by primary evidence) should be allowed as supported by secondary evidence. Here, the Agent is exercising his judgment, and the reviewer may question that judgment. He may believe that the Agent was too lenient, that the secondary evidence does not justify his conclusion. Naturally, the Agent will try to justify his position. In this sense, he has taken up the cudgels for you. If the Agent and the reviewer cannot agree, the chief reviewer will resolve the problem.

*Other tax returns.* Where your return shows income from an estate, trust or partnership, the reviewer makes sure the Agent has checked the estate, trust or partnership return or transfers your case to an Agent who may be examining these returns.

*Prior tax returns.* The Agent may be required to examine the facts on the prior returns and their relationship to the facts shown in this return. He may also look at all subsequently filed returns. Such inquiry may result in the development of hitherto unsuspected facts. The number of ways in which a reviewer may develop new facts depends only on his ingenuity, experience, and zeal. Therefore, remember that even after a waiver is signed, the Agent may ask for additional facts and confront you with new interpretations, raise new issues, or disallow previously allowed items.

You will not be allowed to argue your case directly with the reviewer. But you may be sure that the Agent will present your case in the best light, if for no other reason than to justify his own judgment.

## What to Do if You Disagree with the Examiner

If you disagree with the Agent at the conclusion of an office examination, he will explain the adjustments and appeal procedures available to you. If you think the Agent has taken an unfair position, ask to see his supervisor before the audit is formally closed. You, or your representative, if you hired one, should try to convince the supervisor that the Agent's conclusions are unjustified. If the supervisor agrees with you, better settlement terms may be offered. If the supervisor supports the Agent and you still disagree, you will receive a report of the examination from the District Director and a 30-day letter offering the following alternatives:

1. You can agree to the proposed adjustments and sign an enclosed Form 870;
2. You can request an Appeals Office conference by written protest; or
3. You may ignore the letter, in which case you will eventually receive a statutory notice of deficiency (90-day letter).

If you disagree with the Agent at a field examination, he will prepare and send a complete report explaining fully his proposed adjustments to the district examination review staff for a technical and procedural review. After the review, you will receive a 30-day letter. You now have the following alternatives:

1. You can sign a Form 870 (which precludes appeal to the Tax Court) if you agree with the findings in the report accompanying the letter;
2. You can request an Appeals Office conference by written protest;
3. You can ignore the 30-day letter and wait for the statutory notice of deficiency (90-day letter); or
4. You can pay the tax and file a claim for refund.

## REVIEW OF THE IRS EXAMINATION AND APPEAL STEPS

**Step 1**    **Agent's Examination**
An Agent's examination may find that your return is correct, that you are due a refund, or that you owe an additional amount of tax. If you do not agree to the amount of the refund or additional tax, you have a chance to contest the Agent's finding in a conference.

**Step 2**    **Appeals Office Conference—Regional Director**
If you cannot settle here, you wait for a 90-day letter. Your next appeal step must involve court action.

**Step 3**    **In the Courts**
The 90-day letter gives you 90 days to appeal to the Tax Court. Before trial, you may have an opportunity to settle your case at a hearing with the Appeals Office. If you pay the tax deficiency, you can sue the Government for a refund of taxes in either a Federal District Court or the Claims Court.

The 30-day letter is merely an additional attempt made by the IRS to settle the case without going to trial; since it is not required by the Code, the IRS could dispense with it and send only the 90-day letter. If necessary, you may get additional time to file your protest. However, if the limitation period for the assessment of tax is running out on the tax year in question, you will not get a 30-day letter nor an extension unless a waiver is signed extending the limitation period.

# ───3─

# How to Appeal the Agent's Findings

The law does not require that the Treasury Department provide for appeals within the Internal Revenue Service, but procedures have been developed to give taxpayers an opportunity to get a thorough review of their cases without going to court. Past records have shown that appeals conferences usually result in a settlement; almost 85% of the cases taken to conference are settled. It makes good sense to avail yourself of this comparatively inexpensive and prompt means of settling your tax case. If you file a petition with the Tax Court before going to the Appeals Office for a conference, you will be given a chance to settle before going to trial; in such cases, settlements are obtained about 65% of the time.

The chart below, prepared by the IRS, indicates your appeal options within the IRS and the courts. This chapter will describe the appeal process in detail.

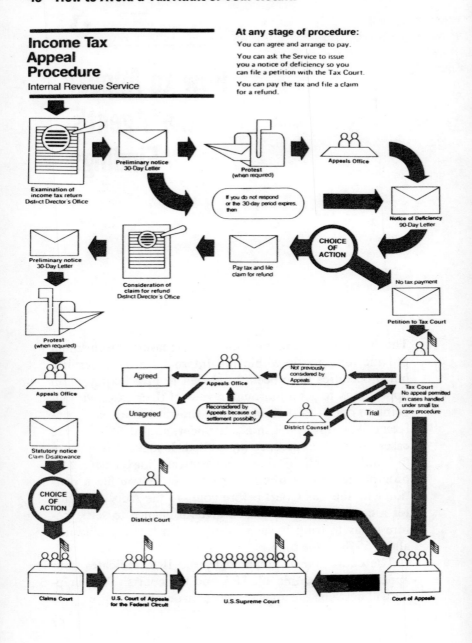

**Income Tax Appeal Procedure**
Internal Revenue Service

**At any stage of procedure:**

You can agree and arrange to pay.

You can ask the Service to issue you a notice of deficiency so you can file a petition with the Tax Court.

You can pay the tax and file a claim for a refund.

Examination of income tax return
District Director's Office

Preliminary notice
30-Day Letter

Protest
(when required)

Appeals Office

If you do not respond or the 30-day period expires, then

Notice of Deficiency
90-Day Letter

CHOICE OF ACTION

Pay tax and file claim for refund

Consideration of claim for refund
District Director's Office

Preliminary notice
30-Day Letter

No tax payment

Petition to Tax Court

Protest
(when required)

Appeals Office

Agreed

Appeals Office

Not previously considered by Appeals

Tax Court
No appeal permitted in cases handled under small tax case procedure

Unagreed

Reconsidered by Appeals because of settlement possibility

District Counsel

Trial

Statutory notice
Claim Disallowance

CHOICE OF ACTION

District Court

Claims Court

U.S. Court of Appeals for the Federal Circuit

U.S. Supreme Court

Court of Appeals

## Should You Ask for a Conference?

Generally, you will have good reason for requesting a conference. You may feel the Agent's authority to accept proposals for settlement is too limited. You may believe he has over-emphasized facts, or disregarded other facts, or failed to give proper weight to them. Perhaps he has misinterpreted applicable tax law or misapplied it to your case. He may even have ignored law that supports your claim.

The very existence of the conference procedure is in itself a recognition of the fact that your objection to the Agent's decision may be right. If the IRS were convinced that the examiner was always correct, there would be no reason for the conferences.

The conference is informal and you are given ample opportunity to present your case. The person who conducts the conference is usually more experienced than the examining agent. He has not prejudged your case. He insists on the facts and applies what appears to be the applicable section of the tax law, or the Commissioner's interpretation as it appears in the Treasury Regulations.

When he has arrived at a conclusion, he will not only tell you what it is, but also explain the basis and reasoning that led him to it.

However, you should be aware of a risk: As you go higher within the IRS, your case will be subject to review by other IRS personnel who may find additional arguments or issues. This risk should be considered in deciding whether to request a conference. A requested conference on a relatively small deficiency may result in a substantial additional deficiency.

Furthermore, on some issues, an administrative appeal to the IRS Appeals Office will generally be fruitless; these are called "appeals coordinated issues," changed periodically by the IRS. On these issues, even if you make a reasonable settlement offer, an IRS auditor or Appeals Officer will stick to his guns and not budge. Here are examples of appeals coordinated issues, current at the time this book went to press:

1. Claiming deductions for tax shelters considered "abusive" by the IRS, as explained in Chapter 1.
2. Claiming a deduction for rental payments on an office building or other property transferred to a trust benefiting members of your family. As part of a gift-lease-back arrangement, you give the property to the trust and then lease it back for use in your business or professional practice. You deduct the lease payments which are reported as income by the lower-bracket trust. The IRS has challenged the deduction but the courts have generally allowed it.
3. Assigning your income and assets to a family trust which pays your living expenses and claims them as deductions. The IRS will disregard the trust and tax you on the income. Courts have supported the IRS and even imposed negligence penalties on those trying to avoid tax on their income by creating the trusts.

## Written Protest Spells Out Your Position

A protest explaining your disagreement with the Agent is required for cases going to the Appeals Office if the case began as a field examination and the amount in issue exceeds $2,500. If your case began as an office examination, or the examination was conducted by correspondence, a written protest is not required, but it would be wise to prepare one if your case involves difficult questions of law or fact. The protest is filed with the District Director who forwards it to the Appeals Office. Instructions for the protest are included in the 30-day letter you received. Chapter 5 explains how to write a protest.

## Do You Need Professional Assistance?

Before proceeding with your case, you should consider whether or not to retain a professional. If you have not yet filed a protest, your counselor will prepare one that will stand up to the scrutiny of the appellate reviewers who are themselves competent, professionally-trained tax experts. You may be represented at the conference by an attorney, CPA or other individual who has passed an examination enabling him to practice before the IRS. You must give your representative a power of attorney.

If you decide to handle the conference on your own, the following pages will help you prepare.

In the Appeals Office, the case is assigned to a conferee. After he acquaints himself with your case, he sets the time of the conference. If it is inconvenient, you can ask for another date or time. An immediate hearing may be granted if you have some unusual reason for it. Depending on your geographic area, the hearing may be held in a Regional Commissioner's Office, District Director's Office, local branch office of the Service, or "on circuit." Conferees sometimes travel to outlying districts to save taxpayers the expense and time involved in a trip to a metropolitan area.

The Appeals Office personnel are specially trained to reach a settlement wherever there is reasonable grounds for one. You can expect them to be courteous and patient but firm where they believe their argument to be strong.

In the majority of cases, neither the Agent nor any other representative of the District Director will attend the conference. If, in a few situations, the Agent does attend a conference, it will be at the invitation of the Appeals Office and only for the purpose of establishing the facts. Since you are appealing from the recommendations of the Agent, do not reargue the case with him. Your sole task will be to convince the Appellate conferee. In all cases, however, you should remember that the Appeals Officer has a copy of the Agent's recommendations and his confidential report, Form T-2, which you never see.

Most Appeals Office conferences take place prior to the issuance of a notice of deficiency. Should a settlement be reached, you will sign a Form 870 or 870-AD (discussed below). Otherwise, a 90-day letter will be issued.

Cases which reach the Appeals Office after the 90-day letter has been issued are known as "90-day cases." Conferences at this stage are not easily granted. You must generally show that you have not had a previous conference for reasons beyond your control, and that there is a reasonable expectation that a settlement can be reached.

If you have petitioned the Tax Court, a second conference may be granted by the Appeals Office as long as it thinks there is some possibility of settlement.

The settlement authority in the Appeals Office is broad. The Appeals Office may trade or split issues where substantial uncertainties exist either in law or in fact, or in both, as to the correct application of the law. It may also settle issues based on its judgment as to the hazards of litigation. The Agents have no authority to consider litigation hazards. One explanation for the reluctance of District Office personnel to close a case is that they realize that another administrative step follows theirs. If they have any doubts about the acceptability of a settlement proposal, they can resolve their doubts by recommending that the case be considered by the Appeals Office. The Appeals Office conferee thinks in terms of the cost and possible result of extended litigation.

Theoretically, nuisance values of a matter are not to be considered, whether they favor the government or you, but as a practical matter, all cases are not entirely free from the influence of a strong bargaining position enjoyed by one of the parties.

You should remember that the Appeals Office conferee considers the case in its entirety. He may find new issues, but they will not be raised arbitrarily or for trading purposes and will be raised only if they have real merit.

## How to Handle the Appeals Office Conference

The conference is held in an informal manner. No stenographic record is made. Your approach to the conference will vary, depending on such facts as whether you wish to settle, whether the issue in dispute is factual or legal, and how strong you feel your case is on a specific issue.

You can assume that the conferee has the Agent's recitation of the facts, his opinions and recommendations, all of which appear in a transmittal memo that you do not receive.

Know the strength and weakness of your position and what you would settle for. If your case is the type that should be settled, the conferee has thought of possible settlements. You should be equally prepared. As a general rule, it is true that a conferee would rather settle cases than send them to the Tax Court, but rarely is he more anxious to settle than you are. To you, the problem represents dollars and cents; to him, a matter of statistics.

You can bring witnesses who will help prove your case or present their statements in affidavit form. Facts brought up for the first time will be referred to the District Director's Office to be checked.

Sufficient time is given you to present your side of the case. Additional hearings are granted as needed.

In a dispute involving a difference of opinion over facts, accept a fair offer from the IRS. You probably will not do any better before the Tax Court and may do worse. If you pay the deficiency and then sue for a refund in the District Court, the facts are decided by a jury that may be sympathetic to your position. In the Tax Court, the facts are determined by judges who may be less sympathetic. Your case is also decided by a judge if you pay the deficiency and sue for a refund in the Claims Court. The odds of winning your case in court are discussed on page 73.

## What Happens After You Propose a Settlement

Your settlement proposal may be accepted or rejected by the Appeals Officer. If accepted, he will ask you to sign either a Form 870 or Form 870-AD. The Form 870 is signed where the settlement is based on a complete agreement with the changes originally recommended by the Agent. On the other hand, where the IRS makes concessions in reaching a settlement in the Appeals Office, a conditional consent, Form 870-AD is signed. Unlike Form 870, which is effective when accepted by the Agent and his supervisor, Form 870-AD does not become effective until it is signed by the Commissioner or his delegate. See the sample copy of Form 870-AD on page 56.

Form 870-AD has been called an informal closing agreement. When you sign it, you agree not to file any claim for refund except for overassessments shown on the agreement form and amounts attributed to a net operating loss carryback deduction. Similarly, the IRS agrees it will not assert any further deficiencies for the year in question except for fraud, malfeasance, concealment or misrepresentation of a material fact, an important mistake in mathematical computation, or an excessive tentative allowance of a net operating loss carryback or investment credit carryback.

The effect of an 870-AD is one-sided. You agree to an immediate assessment of the deficiency, whereas the Treasury does not agree to pay an immediate refund if, for example, the agreement covers two years and one of the years involves an over-assessment. It may, therefore, be advisable to file a protective claim for refund at the same time as the Form 870-AD is signed, or at least be: fore the expiration of the refund period for the year in question. The refund claim should be accompanied by a letter explaining that the purpose of the claim is to protect the taxpayer against an unfavorable disposition of the waiver issue, and that the claim will be withdrawn upon the Treasury's favorable action on the waiver.

Whether or not Form 870-AD is binding on the Treasury and the taxpayer as a closing agreement has been litigated; the decisions present conflicting opinions on the issue.

Filing a Form 870-AD does not stop the running of interest. Interest only stops 30 days after the date the Treasury accepts the form. In any event, the accumulation of interest can be avoided by prepaying the deficiency.

After signing of the Form 870-AD, the Appellate conferee prepares his report.

If the settlement on review is rejected by the Assistant Chief or Associate Chief, he will discuss the case with the Appellate conferee. If the case remains unapproved, you may ask for a hearing before the reviewer who turned down the settlement.

If you do not propose a settlement or the Appellate conferee rejects your proposal, the Appellate conferee prepares his report together with a proposed statutory notice of deficiency. This is sent to an Assistant Chief or Associate Chief for review. If he approves the report, the case is then reviewed by his superior in the Appeals Office. The statutory notice of deficiency is checked by the District Counsel. After final approval by both offices, a 90-day letter is mailed to you. The road is now open for an appeal to the Tax Court.

# 56   How to Avoid a Tax Audit of Your Return

| Form **870-AD**<br>(Rev. October 1983) | DEPARTMENT OF THE TREASURY - INTERNAL REVENUE SERVICE<br>**OFFER OF WAIVER OF RESTRICTIONS ON ASSESSMENT AND COLLECTION<br>OF DEFICIENCY IN TAX AND OF ACCEPTANCE OF OVERASSESSMENT** | |
|---|---|---|
| SYMBOLS | NAME OF TAXPAYER | SSN or EIN |

Pursuant to the provisions of section 6213(d) of the Internal Revenue Code 1954, or corresponding provisions of prior internal revenue laws, the undersigned offers to waive the restrictions provided in section 6213(a) of the Internal Revenue Code of 1954, or corresponding provisions of prior internal revenue laws, and to consent to the assessment and collection of the following deficiencies with interest as provided by law. The undersigned offers also to accept the following overassessments as correct:

### DEFICIENCIES

| YEAR ENDED | KIND OF TAX | TAX | | | | |
|---|---|---|---|---|---|---|
| | | | | | | |
| | | | | | | |
| | | | | | | |
| | | | | | | |
| | | | | | | |
| | | | | | | |
| | | | | | | |

### OVERASSESSMENTS

| YEAR ENDED | KIND OF TAX | TAX | | | | |
|---|---|---|---|---|---|---|
| | | | | | | |
| | | | | | | |
| | | | | | | |
| | | | | | | |
| | | | | | | |
| | | | | | | |
| | | | | | | |

This offer is subject to acceptance for the Commissioner of Internal Revenue. It shall take effect as a waiver of restrictions on the date it is accepted. Unless and until it is accepted, it shall have no force or effect.

If this offer is accepted for the Commissioner, the case shall not be reopened in the absence of fraud, malfeasance, concealment or misrepresentation of material fact, an important mistake in mathematical calculation, or excessive tentative allowances of carrybacks provided by law; and no claim for refund or credit shall be filed or prosecuted for the year(s) stated above other than for amounts attributed to carrybacks provided by law.

| SIGNATURE OF TAXPAYER | DATE |
|---|---|
| SIGNATURE OF TAXPAYER | DATE |
| BY                                          TITLE | DATE |

NOTE.—The execution and filing of this offer will expedite the above adjustment of tax liability. This offer, when executed and timely submitted, will be considered a claim for refund for the above overassessments, as provided in Revenue Ruling 68-65, C.B. 1968-1, 555. It will not, however, constitute a closing agreement under section 7121 of the Internal Revenue Code.

If this offer is executed with respect to a year for which a **JOINT RETURN OF A HUSBAND AND WIFE** was filed, it must be signed by both spouses unless one spouse, acting under a power of attorney, signs as agent for the other.

If the taxpayer is a corporation, the offer shall be signed with the corporate name followed by the signature and title of the officers authorized to sign.

This offer may be executed by the taxpayer's attorney or agent provided this action is specifically authorized by a power of attorney which, if not previously filed, must accompany the form.

| FOR<br>INTERNAL<br>REVENUE<br>USE ONLY | DATE ACCEPTED FOR COMMISSIONER | SIGNATURE |
|---|---|---|
| | OFFICE | TITLE |

## What to Do After Receiving a 90-Day Letter

Before the IRS can assess a deficiency, it must send by registered or certified mail a statutory notice of deficiency, called a "90-day letter." It gives you the chance, within 90 days from the date of its mailing, to appeal to the Tax Court of the United States. If you live outside of the United States, you are allowed 150 days. In the event the 90th or 150th day falls on a Saturday or Sunday, or on a legal holiday in the District of Columbia, you have until the next business day to file a petition with the Tax Court.

You receive a 90-day letter at the end of the period allowed in the 30-day letter if you have not signed a Form 870 or filed a formal protest, or after a hearing with the Appeals Office. At the end of the 90 (or 150) days, the deficiency is assessed.

On receipt of the 90-day letter, you can do one of the following:

1. File a petition with the Tax Court. No assessment can be made until its decision becomes final;
2. Do nothing and wait for the assessment of the deficiency; or
3. Sign the Form 870. This limits the interest on the deficiency. You can still take your case to the Tax Court, or you can pay the disputed deficiency and file a refund claim. After it is rejected, you can sue in a Federal District Court or the Claims Court.

For a deficiency involving a joint return, the 90-day letter is mailed as a single joint notice. The IRS will send a duplicate original of the joint notice to both you and your wife if it is notified of separate addresses.

The IRS may issue more than one 90-day letter for the same year before the earliest of the following events: (1) Expiration of the assessment period; (2) execution of a final closing agreement or compromise; or (3) filing of a timely petition to the Tax Court. You have 90 days from the date of the Treasury's mailing of the deficiency notice to petition the Tax Court for review.

## Getting a Settlement After Appealing to the Tax Court

You may still be able to get a settlement even after you have filed a petition in the Tax Court. If you have brought your case to the Tax Court without first appealing to the Appeals Office for a conference to settle the dispute, you will be asked to discuss a settlement with the Appeals Office. Your case may be referred to the Appeals Office for settlement by the District Counsel's Office for up to six months if the deficiency is $10,000 or less, with a possible extension where a settlement is considered likely.

Even if you have filed a Tax Court petition after an unsuccessful conference in the Appeals Office, your case will still be referred back to the Appeals Office for settlement unless the District Counsel determines that there is little likelihood of a settlement. The Appeals Office may enter into a binding settlement. If the case is returned to the Counsel's Office, it determines whether to settle or proceed to trial.

## Informal Procedures for Small Claims Cases in Tax Court

If you decide to take your case to the Tax Court, there is a special procedure for hearing deficiencies under $10,000, available at your option. It permits a more flexible, informal, and expeditious handling of small claims than is allowed under the usual court rules. At the time this book went to press, the filing fee for a small claims case was only $10, compared to the regular $60 Tax Court filing fee. Many taxpayers with small claims file petitions *pro se,* that is, without representation by an attorney. You may be represented by a non-attorney only if he has passed a special Tax Court exam. Cases may be heard by commissioners rather than by judges, an innovation that may make speedier hearings possible. During the trial of a small claims case, the Court may order that the small case rules be discontinued and that the usual Court rules be followed because the issues require a more formal hearing, or it becomes clear that the $10,000 jurisdiction limit will be exceeded. Once a small claims decision is rendered, it is final and not subject to appeal by either party. The loss of a right to appeal is a risk you must weigh before taking the "small claims" route.

## Penalty for Filing Frivolous Tax Court Suit

The Tax Court may impose a penalty of up to $5,000 if it concludes that you have filed a case merely to delay your payment of tax, or that your position is clearly frivolous. The purpose of the penalty is to deter the filing of Tax Court petitions where the taxpayer's arguments have been repeatedly rejected in earlier decisions—for example, claiming war protester deductions or assigning income to a sham church which deducts your personal living costs.

# 4

# How to Analyze Your Tax Dispute

You should have a clear idea why the Internal Revenue Service disputes a particular item on your tax return.

Has an item been questioned because you cannot prove that you spent the amount claimed? Or has it been questioned because you cannot, as a matter of law, claim the item?

The results of the disallowance are the same, but your ability to contest the decision is different depending on the reason for the disallowance.

In the first case, you must bring evidence, such as checks and bills, to prove facts. In the second case, you may not have any room for an argument because your case does not come within the law permitting you to claim the item.

For example, Garcon, an American citizen, supports his mother, a French citizen who lives in Paris, France. He has complete records of all the money he has sent her. She had no other source of support. Garcon claims her as an exemption on his return.

Brown, an American citizen, also claims his mother, who is an American citizen, as an exemption. She lives alone in a small apartment. Brown has checks totaling $1,000 paid to her for support.

The returns of both Garcon and Brown are examined and their exemption claims for their mothers are disallowed.

Garcon's is disallowed because his mother does not meet the citizenship or residence test for dependents.

Brown's is disallowed because, on examination, the Agent learns that his mother received Social Security of $1,100. The Agent argued that she spent that amount on her own support and as it exceeded the $1,000 contributed by Brown, he is not entitled to claim her as an exemption.

Garcon has no grounds on which to dispute an Agent. He has not met the terms of the law which require a dependent to be a U.S. citizen or resident, or a resident of Canada or Mexico. He will gain nothing by arguing or carrying his dispute further. The law simply does not allow an exemption for a foreign citizen living abroad, other than Canadian or Mexican residents. On the other hand, Brown has met all the terms of the law except the requirement for proving support of his mother. He claims he has met the law. Actually, he may have, but he must prove his case. He has shown he gave $1,000; he needs to prove an additional expenditure of at least $100.01 more. Perhaps he gave this amount in cash, or paid a bill for her directly. His problem is to convince the Agent of these facts.

## When the Law Is Not Clear

Issues as presented by the cases of Brown and Garcon are easy to define, but you may be involved in a case in which the law is not clear, or there is dispute between the IRS and the courts on how a particular law is to be interpreted.

For example, the IRS and some courts disagree over whether a professional or businessman may use a gift-leaseback of the building to shift income to a family trust.

Let us assume that a physician who owns the office building in which his office is located makes a gift of the building to a family trust and then leases back space to use for an office. The desired tax result: The physician deducts his rental payments made to the trust; the trust, which will be in a lower tax bracket than he is, reports the rental income on its trust return. The IRS will generally disallow the physician's rental deduction on the grounds that there is no business purpose for the overall transaction. However, the Tax Court and several appeals courts have allowed the deduction, as long as an independent trustee is appointed and a reasonable rent is charged. These courts hold that the business purpose requirement is satisfied because the leaseback provides office space. On the other hand, some appeals courts have supported the IRS position. Since the IRS is not bound to follow contrary court decisions, a professional or businessman using a gift-leaseback is forced to go to the expense of taking the matter to a "friendly" court that has allowed the rental deduction.

## Who Has the Last Word?

Generally speaking, the average tax problems of an individual taxpayer involve relatively simple factual and legal questions. Most often, the examination will require the presentation of evidence to support the reporting of an item. Here, as you can see, there is no need to argue the "law."

But if you have to argue the "law," you must be able to cite accurately the authority for the statement you make. In a dispute, the Agent will argue that the IRS policy is the "law," while the taxpayer may present a court decision to the contrary.

Even where the Agent might be pursuaded to accept a court's interpretation, your case may differ factually from the decision on which you are relying. We have given you an example involving gift-leasebacks of an office building. A court decision may have allowed a deduction for rentals on the leaseback where an independent trustee was appointed. If you have entered a gift-leaseback arrangement but a relative is selected as trustee, and there is evidence that you are paying less than a fair-market rental, the court decision will not help your case.

Sometimes an Agent will question an item that you have reported correctly on the basis of a rule or regulation with which he is not familiar. The Agent may force you to find the specific regulation and present it as authority before the item is allowed.

At this point, it is important to have an understanding of the sources and the structure of the tax law. You should be aware that the language of the material you will be dealing with is written by attorneys for attorneys, and at times is even difficult for them to understand. But if you have decided to represent yourself, you must know the sources of the law with which you will be dealing. They are required for an analysis and understanding of the strength of your position. If you find the subject too difficult, it may be better to give your case to an attorney.

## WHAT MAKES UP THE TAX LAW

### The Internal Revenue Code

The Internal Revenue Code of 1954, as passed by Congress, is the present statutory foundation of the federal income tax law. The title of the Code remains fixed with the date 1954, although sections of the Code are amended frequently.

Locating the Code authority for the treatment of an item is often only the beginning. Many laws are written in broad, general words. To understand the practical meaning of these words, you may have to review IRS regulations, rulings, and court decisions.

## IRS Regulations

IRS regulations have the force and effect of law. Your failure to comply with a regulation can result in a negligence penalty. However, the validity of a regulation can be questioned by a taxpayer in a court action. Courts are not bound by the regulations and can overrule them if they are found to be contrary to the terms of the section they attempt to interpret. But once a regulation has interpreted a Code provision, passage of a similar law with the exact wording is often regarded by the courts as evidence that Congress is satisfied with the regulation and thus the regulation will not generally be overruled. Even if a regulation is disapproved, the Service can continue to enforce the regulation unless reversal of the regulation is by the Supreme Court.

Each section of the regulations is preceded by the section, subsection, or paragraph of the 1954 Internal Revenue Code which it interprets. The sections of the regulations are distinguished from sections of the Code by the Arabic numeral 1, followed by a decimal point (.) before the corresponding section number for the provision of the Internal Revenue Code. This designation is then followed by a dash (-) and a number further identifying a section of the regulation. With these numbers you can find regulations interpreting a Code provision. Thus, the regulation explaining IRC Section 301 is designated 1.301, and a section of that regulation is identified as 1.301-1.

## Revenue Rulings

Revenue rulings make up a large body of IRS interpretations of the tax law. They are essentially official replies to specific problems raised by taxpayers and do not have the force and effect of formal regulations. Despite this limitation, they can be used as general guidelines of the Service position. IRS officials will follow the rulings in cases having similar facts to those presented in the rulings.

Revenue rulings are published weekly in the Internal Revenue Bulletin. Every half-year, these rulings are republished in a book, called Cumulative Bulletin, available to the public at the Government Printing Office.

References to Revenue rulings appear as follows:

In the weekly Internal Revenue Bulletin, Rev. Rul. 82-166, IRB 1982-40,9. This means that the particular ruling in 1982 is numbered as 166, it appears in the 40th weekly bulletin of that year, and in that bulletin, can be found on page 9.

In the Cumulative Bulletin, Rev. Rul. 82-166, 1982-2 CB 190. This means that the ruling appears in the second half-year Cumulative Bulletin for 1982 and in that book can be found on page 190.

## Other IRS Rulings and Releases

After the Revenue rulings, there are several other Service releases and rulings helpful in determining Service policy:

1. Letter Rulings. These include private rulings, determination letters, and technical advice memoranda. Virtually all letter rulings are open to public inspection after all information that could identify the taxpayer involved has been deleted. Letter rulings may not be used as a precedent in other cases by either the IRS or other taxpayers. However, they may be helpful as they reflect the IRS' policy and interpretation of the law. Letter rulings are referred to by a seven number citation: The first two numbers indicate the year; the next two numbers, the week of

the year the ruling is issued; the last three numbers, the letter ruling numbers in sequence for that week. For example, Letter Ruling 7821098 was issued in the 21st week of 1978; it was the 98th letter ruling of that week.

2. Revenue Procedures. These describe internal practices and procedures within the Service. They are published in the Internal Revenue Bulletin. References to them are prefixed by the abbreviations Rev. Proc.

3. Technical Information Releases and Announcements. These describe current Service policy toward a specific issue. They are designed primarily for public release. Newspaper reports of Service policy usually stem from Technical Information Releases. Sometimes a Technical Information Release will be republished as a Revenue ruling.

4. General Counsel Memoranda, Actions on Decisions, and Technical Memoranda. These are internal IRS documents. General Counsel's Memoranda (GCM's) are legal opinions on proposed revenue rulings and technical advice memoranda. Actions on Decisions (AOD's) recommend whether or not to appeal adverse court decisions. Technical Memoranda (TM's) indicate the legal and policy basis for proposed Treasury regulations. These documents are released to the public after deletions are made by the IRS to remove identifying information.

## Court Decisions

Court decisions are important authority, but to use them effectively, you must know the extent of their authority within the federal judicial system and their effect upon the IRS.

The IRS is not bound to follow a court decision in any case other than in the specific case in which the decision has been written. The only exceptions to this rule are decisions of the Supreme Court.

Courts are not bound to follow the decision of another court. Again, the only exceptions are Supreme Court decisions.

Court decisions are not of equal weight. A decision of the Tax Court has substantially greater significance than a decision rendered by a Federal District Court and often by a Federal Court of Appeals, primarily because the Tax Court hears cases all over the nation and will apply its decisions on a nationwide basis.

Federal District Courts are local federal courts and a Court of Appeals hears appeals only on a regional basis. So where one decision of the Tax Court will be equally applied through the United States, there may be several conflicting interpretations among district courts in various localities and Courts of Appeals in the various geographical regions. For example, a District Court in California is not bound to follow a decision handed down by a District Court in New York; and a Court of Appeals for one region is not bound to follow a decision of a Court of Appeals for another region. However, the precedent of a Tax Court decision rendered in New York will be controlling authority in a Tax Court hearing held anywhere else in the United States.

## Supreme Court Decisions

Supreme Court decisions are the only decisions which the Internal Revenue Service and lower courts are required to follow. They have the same force as the Code and remain in force until Congress specifically changes the Court's interpretation or the Supreme Court in a later decision reverses its own position.

Here as an example of a reference to a Supreme Court decision: Beulah Crane, 331 U.S. 1 (1947). Beulah Crane is the name of the taxpayer involved in the case: 331 refers to the official volume in which the case is found; U.S. designates the official Supreme Court volumes; 1, to the page within the volume; 1947, to the year of the decision. The case can also be found in volumes by private publishers such as Commerce Clearing House and Prentice Hall.

## Courts of Appeals Decisions

There are 12 U.S. Courts of Appeals that hear appeals taken by either taxpayers or the IRS from decisions rendered by the Tax Court or Federal District Court. Eleven of these are regional courts that hear cases arising within their region, which is technically called a circuit; the twelfth hears cases arising within the District of Columbia. The circuits and the states within each circuit are listed on page 69. A separate appeals court hears appeals from decisions of the Claims Court.

Courts of Appeals decisions make up an important part of Federal tax law, but the effectiveness of a particular decision may vary because of these facts:

1. The Internal Revenue Service is not bound to follow any precedent set by an appeals court decision.
2. The Tax Court does not consider itself bound to follow any precedent set by an appeals court decision. The Tax Court view is that its nationwide jurisdiction cannot be restricted by the rules of the twelve different appeals courts. However, it will generally follow an appeals court decision in the circuit to which the current Tax Court case is appealable.
3. A Court of Appeals of one region is not bound to follow the precedent of a Court of Appeals in another region. Consequently, a decision of a particular ap-

peals court is far stronger for taxpayers who, by virtue of their residence, can bring their appeals before that court than for taxpayers who must appeal to other appeals courts. A court will generally follow its own precedents unless it is overruled or later decides its original position was wrong.

Courts of Appeals' decisions are referred to their place in the Federal Series reports published by the West Publishing Company. The first series is cited as "F."; the second series, as "F. 2d", which began in 1924. For example, take the citation Steffens, 707 F. 2d 478 (11th Cir.,

## STATES WITHIN COURT OF APPEALS REGIONS

**First Circuit**
Maine
Massachusetts
New Hampshire
Rhode Island
Puerto Rico

**Second Circuit**
Connecticut
New York
Vermont

**Third Circuit**
Delaware
New Jersey
Pennsylvania
Virgin Islands

**District of Columbia**

**Fourth Circuit**
Maryland
North Carolina
South Carolina
Virginia
West Virginia

**Fifth Circuit**
Canal Zone
Louisiana
Mississippi
Texas

**Sixth Circuit**
Kentucky
Michigan
Ohio
Tennessee

**Seventh Circuit**
Illinois
Indiana
Wisconsin

**Eighth Circuit**
Arkansas
Iowa
Minnesota
Missouri
Nebraska
North Dakota
South Dakota

**Ninth Circuit**
Alaska
Arizona
California
Hawaii
Idaho
Montana
Nevada
Oregon
Washington
Guam
Northern Mariana
   Islands

**Tenth Circuit**
Colorado
Kansas
New Mexico
Oklahoma
Utah
Wyoming

**Eleventh Circuit**
Alabama
Florida
Georgia

1983): Steffens is the name of the taxpayer; 707, the volume of the second series of Federal Reporter; 478, the page within that volume; 11th Cir., the Circuit of the Appeals Court deciding the case; and 1983, the year of decision.

The Treasury will sometimes announce its decision to follow or not to follow a Court of Appeals decision. It may also publish an appeals court opinion in the weekly Internal Revenue Bulletin as a "Court Decision." This action can be construed as Treasury approval of the court's conclusion.

## U.S. Tax Court

The Tax Court is a special court for taxpayers who appeal tax deficiencies imposed by the IRS for income, estate, or gift taxes. It is independent of the Treasury. Its members are called judges, and its decisions are subject to the same judicial review as that of any other federal court. They can be appealed to a Court of Appeals and then to the Supreme Court. The Tax Court's policy is to follow decisions of the U.S. Court of Appeals to which the appeal in the case before it could be taken. For example, if the Tax Court is deciding a case which is appealable to the Court of Appeals for the Fifth Circuit, the Tax Court will follow a Fifth Circuit decision which involves the same factual and legal issues.

Between 1924 and 1942, the Court was known as the Board of Tax Appeals. Cases decided by the Court before 1942 are referred to, for example, as 20 BTA 45; cases afterward, as 30 T.C. 43. (The first number refers to the volume of the particular series of Court decisions; the second number, to the page on which the case is found.)

The Internal Revenue Service is not bound by a Tax Court decision except in the case in which the decision has been rendered. It can continue to litigate the same issue in other cases before the Tax Court and in other courts. However, in a tax dispute with a taxpayer involving the same issue in which the Court decided against the Treasury, the Service may be more inclined to negotiate a settlement than to have the taxpayer bring his case before the Tax Court again.

There are two types of Tax Court decisions:

*Regular decisions.* These are officially reported in bound volumes. They are recognized by the abbreviation T.C., located between the volume number and the page number.

*Memorandum decisions.* These are not collected in official volumes but are released in mimeographed form, copies of which go to the litigants. Private tax publishing services reprint memorandum decisions.

What is the Court test for reporting a case as either a regular decision or a memorandum decision? The Court says a memorandum decision involves no question of law but merely facts that the Court believes are limited to a number of cases. If a memorandum decision does involve a question of law, the question is usually one that has been decided previously by the Tax Court and followed by the Court of Appeals. However, taxpayers can and do appeal memorandum decisions to the Court of Appeals, just as they appeal reported decisions. Since April 8, 1954, the Tax Court has followed a practice of giving official numbers to the memorandum decisions according to the year they were rendered, such as T.C. Memo 1960-2.

How important are memorandum decisions? Although these are considered minor decisions by the Court, this should not discourage you from using them. Most Tax Court decisions are memorandum decisions. They provide useful examples of Tax Court policy toward a particular tax issue. Furthermore, memorandum decisions are often appealed and the decisions of the Appeals Court in these cases may become important authority.

The Treasury follows a policy of announcing its acceptance of, or disagreement with, a Tax Court holding against a position held by the IRS in an officially reported decision. No policy statements are made for memorandum decisions. These announcements are made in the weekly Internal Revenue Bulletin, as acquiescences or nonacquiescences. The IRS cautions that an acquiescence of a particular decision merely signifies its acceptance of the Tax Court's conclusion. It does not necessarily mean that the IRS has accepted or approved of the Court's reasons for the conclusion, and it advises its officials to apply the rule of acquiesced cases only to cases that have substantially the same facts and circumstances as the acquiesced case. An acquiescence of a reported case is recognized by the abbreviation (Acq.) at the end of the case citation. However, if you are going to rely on an acquiesced case, try to find the exact terms of the IRS approval from the weekly Internal Revenue Bulletin or Cumulative Bulletin. Sometimes an acquiescence is limited to only one particular issue of a case. Finally, the IRS is free to withdraw an acquiescence or nonacquiescence.

## Federal District Court

There is at least one Federal District Court for each state; the more populous states have two or more district courts. A Federal District Court can hear only tax cases in which a taxpayer sues for a refund after his claim has been denied by the Treasury.

Generally, a District Court opinion is not strong authority, primarily because of the local nature of a District Court. However, a well-reasoned District Court decision may be accepted by other courts and even the Treasury, and in absence of any other authority on a particular issue, a decision of a District Court may prove helpful because it presents at least one published view of the problem.

District Court decisions are reported in the Federal Supplement series published by the West Publishing Company. For example, take the case of Smith, (DC) 32 F. Supp. 891. Smith is the name of the taxpayer, (DC) refers to the fact that the opinion is from a District Court, 32 is the volume number of the Federal Supplement series, and 891 is the page within that volume.

## U.S. Claims Court

There is only one United States Claims Court. It is located in Washington, D.C. and hears only suits for refund of taxes. Decisions by the Claims Court on income tax questions are not numerous and have not had an important effect on the development of the income tax law. However, you might be encouraged to choose the Claims Court to hear your case if there had been a favorable decision on an issue you may be disputing with the Treasury. And a well-reasoned Claims Court decision may be followed by other courts.

Appeals from Claims Court decisions are heard by a special Appeals Court, the U.S. Court of Appeals for the Federal Circuit.

## Odds of Winning a Court Case

If you cannot reach a settlement with the IRS and you take your case to court, the odds favor the IRS. For example, in 1983 the IRS won about 64% of the regular Tax Court cases; taxpayers won only about 5% with the balance being partial victories for each side. Taxpayers did slightly better under the informal "small tax" procedures for deficiencies of $5,000 or less. The IRS won about 56% of these cases, taxpayers 8% and the balance partial victories for each side. If you pay the disputed tax and sue for a refund in either a federal district court or the Claims Court your chances of winning a complete victory are much higher than in the Tax Court. Taxpayers won about 37% of the 1983 District Court and 50% of the Claims Court cases.

If you appeal a decision of the Tax Court or a Federal District Court to a U.S. Court of Appeals, your odds of winning are much lower than in the lower courts. In 1983, the IRS won approximately 80% of the decisions, taxpayers 14%, with the balance, partial victories for each side.

# —5

# How to Write Your Protest

The protest is simply your written explanation of the reasons for your disagreement with the Agent. In it, you give the conferee who will hear the appeal your side of the dispute.

There is no special form for the protest. The important thing is to include information and arguments that present your case in the best light.

A sample protest appears in this chapter on page 78.

## What Information Must Be Put into the Protest?

Include in the protest:

1. Your name and address.
2. Date and symbols on the 30-day letter.
3. Years covered and the amounts of tax liability in dispute for each year. List here only the amount of the proposed deficiency.
4. An itemized schedule of the Agent's findings with which you disagree. Make sure you cover every item

you contest. Where more than one finding is involved, list each one separately and number it.

5. A statement of facts supporting your position in each of the items named in (4). If you disagreed with more than one of the Agent's findings in (4), state your position in numbered paragraphs which correspond to the schedule in (4).

6. A statement of the law on which you rely for each item listed in (4). Use separate paragraphs numbered to correspond with the items in (4).

7. Request for a conference with the Appeals Office, if desired. If you do not make the request in the protest, you will get no hearing, and the case will be decided exclusively on the basis of what you submit as your protest.

The most important part of the protest is the presentation of your arguments. You can divide the presentation into three parts:

A. A numbered summary of arguments.
B. A statement of facts covering the disputed items.
C. A careful development of arguments, supported by citations of legal authority.

The last step, supporting your argument with legal authorities, may be the most difficult part of preparing your protest. Even if you did not retain a tax professional to represent you at the audit, you probably now need a tax expert to prepare a persuasive legal argument. If you attempt to represent yourself, you must be able to research the legal issues and cite the legal authorities described in Chapter 4.

Separate protests do not have to be filed if more than one tax year is involved. All the tax years covered in the 30-day letter can be included in one protest.

An original and a copy of the protest must be filed.

## How to Sign the Protest

You must declare the statement of facts presented in your protest (Step (4) above) to be true under penalties of perjury; to do this, include the following statement at the end of your protest:

"Under penalties of perjury, I declare that the facts presented in my written protest, which are set out in the accompanying statement of facts, schedules, and other attached statements, are to the best of my knowledge and belief, true, correct, and complete."

If you are being represented, a substitute declaration should be included, indicating that the representative has prepared the protest and accompanying documents, and stating that the protest and accompanying documents are true to the best of the representative's knowledge.

## Writing Suggestions

Stress the equities of your case. A case that shows that a decision against you would be unfair may be stronger than one in which the technicalities are on your side.

Write the facts so that they can be understood. They should be clear and accurate. List them in the order in which they happened.

Do not omit those facts that seem to be against you. When explained, they may not be as detrimental to your case as they first appeared.

Substantiate the facts with exhibits, affidavits, or any other proof.

Try to avoid unimportant facts which are not relevant to the issue. Make sure you understand how the principles of law relate to the facts you state. Otherwise, your argument will be weak.

## SAMPLE PROTEST LETTER

May 1, 1983

District Director of Internal Revenue
Audit Division
P.O. Box 3100
New York, N.Y. 10015

> *PROTEST: In the Matter of Richard and Ruth Roe:*
> *Calendar Year Ended 1981*

Sir:

Receipt is acknowledged of your letter dated April 7, 1983 transmitting the report of Internal Revenue Agent Robert Smith which recommends a deficiency in income tax for the taxable calendar year 1981.

The taxpayers protest the finding and determination set forth in the report and submit the following in protest:

(a) The taxpayers are Richard and Ruth Roe and their address is 1 Somm Place, Suburban Center, N.Y.

(b) The letter transmitting the Revenue Agent's report is dated April 7, 1983 and bears the symbols Au: X:30D.

(c) The year involved is the taxable calendar year 1981.

(d) The taxpayers take exception to the finding that they are not entitled to a deduction of $1,000 for their son, Ronald.

(e) The grounds upon which the taxpayers rely are as follows:

*The Facts*

Ronald Roe, the taxpayers' son was 20 years old and resided with the taxpayers during the entire year '1981. Data was submitted to the examining officer (and is incorporated herein by reference) demonstrating that the taxpayers were the sole contributing support of their son during 1981.

During the period beginning July 15, 1981 and ending

September 15, 1981, Ronald worked as a loader for the
Y & Z Company, receiving a salary of $1,004. However,
in order to work at this job, he was required to supply
his own work clothing consisting of:

| | |
|---|---:|
| 2 pairs coveralls—cost | $32.50 |
| 1 pair rubber soled shoes—cost | 10.95 |
| Total | $43.45 |

Thus, the income earned by Ronald during 1981 was
only $960.55.

*The Issue*

The examining officer determined that since Ronald's
salary was in excess of $1,000 for the year 1981, the tax-
payers were not entitled to the dependency exemption of
$1,000.

The taxpayers maintain that for purposes of Section
151 of the 1954 Internal Revenue Code, the gross income of their son for the year 1981 was $960.55. There-
fore, they are entitled to the exemption provided in that
section.

*Law and Argument*

Section 151(e)(1)(A) provides that there shall be allowed an exemption of $1,000 for each dependent "whose
gross income for the calendar year in which the taxable
year of the taxpayer begins is less than $1,000."

Section 152(a)(1) defines "dependent" as:

". . . any of the following individuals over half of
whose support for the calendar year in which the taxable
year of the taxpayer begins was received from the taxpayer (or . . .):

"(1) a son . . . of the taxpayer . . ."

Since Ronald fits the definition of "dependent" as set
forth in the Internal Revenue Code, the sole issue is
whether his earnings during 1981 were $1,000 or over, or
whether they were less than $1,000.

The situation here is similar to that in *John B. Rives,*
T.C. Memo. Op. Dec. 7, 1949. In that case, a dependent
son worked as a newsboy. His earnings exceeded the

gross income test by $.38. However, he incurred expense of $2.50 for repairs to his bicycle which he used in his work. It was conceded by the Commissioner and held by the Court that the taxpayer was entitled to the dependency deduction for his son.

In view of the above decision, and the concession by the Commissioner, which established his position towards this issue, the taxpayers maintain that the examining officer erred in disallowing the dependency exemption.

A conference is requested before the Appeals Office where this matter may be discussed.

Respectfully submitted,

"Under penalties of perjury, we declare that the statement of facts presented in this protest and in any accompanying schedules and statements has been examined by us and to the best of our knowledge and belief is true, correct, and complete."

---

Discuss the issues in the order of their importance. Leave the least important for last. Say what and who are involved.

Write short headings before each issue; they must accurately state the point you are making. Repeat important facts if they help in understanding your argument.

Summarize the point you are making and show how it applies to your case.

Sometimes a short quotation from a leading case is effective if you can relate the case to your facts, but avoid long quotations from many cases.

Be sure that every case you cite stands for what you say it does.

Try to put yourself in the place of the conferee who is going to read the protest. Ask yourself what you would want to know in such a case in order to answer the questions and then try to supply the information.

Be brief; a well-organized, succinct and interesting protest will help you.

Consider the appearance of the letter. Make it appealing. Use side heads to break up solid pages of type. Sometimes graphs, photographs, charts and other illustrations help make your point in an interesting and attractive manner.

## You File a Protest in Your District Director's Office

You file the original and one duplicate copy of the protest. No filing fee is necessary. If you are appealing to the Appeals Office, the District Director sends the protest along with your case to the Appeals Office.

Some District Directors have set up "screening groups" to review protests before they are sent to the Appeals Office. If, after reading a protest, a reviewer believes that there is a basis for settlement, he will refer the case back to the Examination Division for settlement. For this reason, make sure that your protest presents the case well so that a reviewer can have a basis for his decision.

## How the Appeals Office Operates

The Appeals Office is completely divorced, functionally and physically, from the District Director's office which supervised the audit of your return. This segregation is not accidental; its major purpose is to provide an appellate procedure which, organizationally at least, will tend to produce free and unbiased opinions. An Appeals Officer is not responsible to the District Director (who controls the Revenue Agent and his supervisor), so he is less likely to be unduly influenced by the conclusions reached in that office and more likely to make his decisions objectively. The Appeals Officer does not need, nor does he seek, the approval of the Revenue Agent, Supervisor, or District Director for any decision he may make.

# 6

# Time Limits Within Which the Service Must Act

The Service normally begins a tax examination within a year after a return was filed. It may happen that the audit of a return filed for a recent year leads to an examination of a return for an earlier year. The authority of the IRS to examine returns of prior years is restricted by statutes of limitation. Generally, the IRS has three years after the date on which your tax return is filed to proceed against you. However, when you file a return before the due date, the period does not start from the filing date but from the due date. For example, instead of filing your last quarterly estimated tax payment on January 15, you file a final return on January 31. The limitation period on the final return begins on April 15, which is the due date, not on January 31, the date you filed.

To start the running of the statute of limitations, the District Director or your regional Service Center must receive your return. A filing with any other Treasury office does not start the statute.

In any controversy concerning the statute, you must prove that you filed a return. If you fail to do this, there is no limit on the time during which the Government can make an assessment against you. Similarly, filing a return containing insufficient information of your tax liability does not start the running of the statute.

There are several exceptions to the general rule that the filing of a return starts the running of the statutory period.

Where a false or fraudulent return is filed with intent to evade tax, tax may be assessed at any time, even if an amended nonfraudulent return is later filed.

Where a willful attempt in any manner is made to defeat or evade tax, the tax may be assessed at any time.

Where no return is filed, the tax may be assessed at any time.

## If More than 25% of Gross Income Is Omitted

If you omit an amount which is more than 25% of the gross income shown on your return, the IRS may make an assessment within six years after the return is filed, rather than three years. For example, in a 1982 return (which was filed on April 15, 1983) gross income of $5,000 is reported, but a $2,000 gain from the sale of a home has been omitted. In this case, the IRS has until April 15, 1989, to assess a deficiency on the 1982 return. The reason: The omitted $2,000 gain is more than 25% of the gross income reported on the return (25% of $5,000 or $1,250). However, take the same set of facts except that gross income is $10,000. Here, the three-year statute applies rather than the six-year statute because the omission is not more than 25% of the reported gross income (25% of $10,000 or $2,500).

To apply the six-year statute, the IRS has the burden of proving that there is an omission and that it exceeds 25% of the reported gross income. If it fails to sustain its claim, the three-year statute applies. To be successful against such a claim, you must show that the items were not omitted; for example, that the item was tax free or not taxable in the particular year or that the Treasury's valuation is incorrect. You may not base your defense on a plea of an honest mistake or the use of an incorrect method of accounting, or claim that the omission was reduced to less than 25% by an amended return. The six-year statute runs from the filing of the original return. The filing of an amended return does not shorten the six-year period.

In figuring gross income, do not confuse the way income is reported on a tax return with the concept of gross income. For example, when reporting capital gains and losses, the net gain or loss is reported on a return. But this amount is not gross income. For purposes of computing the gross income omission, gross income would include the capital gains before they are reduced by either capital losses or by the 60% deduction for long-term capital gains, or by both. Where you have a trade or business, gross income means the total amount received from the sale of goods or services. This amount is not to be reduced by the cost of such goods or services. Gross income with respect to a partner's share of partnership income means the partner's share of the partnership gross income and not partnership net income.

If you omit a questionable item from gross income, you can prevent an extension of the statute by adequately disclosing the fact of the omission on the return or in an attached statement. If the disclosure adequately tells the Treasury of the nature and amount of the item omitted, that item will not be counted in determining whether there has been an omission of more than 25% of gross income.

There are special limitation rules in the following cases:

*Where separate returns were originally filed and later a joint return is filed,* the starting date of the limitation period depends on whether both spouses originally filed separately.

*Where both spouses previously filed separate returns,* the period begins on the last date that either spouse could have filed a separate return.

*Where only one spouse filed a return because the other had gross income under the requirement for filing a return,* the period begins on the last date that the spouse who filed could have filed his return.

*Where only one spouse filed a return, even though the other had gross income requiring the filing of a return,* the period begins when they file the joint return.

The regular three-year limitation period is figured from the starting dates shown above but must extend to at least one year after the actual filing date of the joint return. Thus, if the three-year limitation period expires before one year after the joint return's filing date, the limitation period is extended until the end of that one year.

*Where an involuntary conversion has occurred,* tax on the gain can be deferred by investing the proceeds in similar property. When tax on gain has been deferred, the three-year period starts when the District Director is notified that the property has been replaced or that no replacement has been made. If a replacement is made before the beginning of the last year in which any part of the gain is received on the conversion, then the limitation period for any year before that year (during which the election to replace was in effect) ends when the limitation period for the last year ends. Failure to notify the District Director prevents the statute from closing.

*Where a residence is sold and a new one is bought within two years before or after the sale, part or all of the gain may not be taxed.* The three-year period of limitations on assessments does not begin until the District Director is notified that a new residence is bought, giving its cost, or that no residence has been bought within the time limit.

## When the Running of the Statute Is Suspended

The limitation period is automatically suspended in the following cases:

*When a 90-day letter is sent,* the period of limitation is automatically suspended for 150 days. (Technically, this includes the 90-day period during which the IRS cannot assess a deficiency, plus an additional 60 days afterwards.) However, if the period would have expired during the suspended period, the IRS cannot assess an additional deficiency after that time though it can still assess the first deficiency.

*If you take a case to the Tax Court,* the period is extended until the Tax Court's decision becomes final and for 60 days afterwards.

*Where there is a bankruptcy or a receivership,* the period is extended from the period beginning with the date of the institution of bankruptcy or receivership proceedings until 30 days after the Commissioner in Washington is notified of the receivership or bankruptcy. The period cannot be extended for more than two years because of bankruptcy or receivership.

*Where assets are in the custody or control of a court,* the period of limitation is suspended for the period in which the assets are in the hands of the court and for six months thereafter.

*When a taxpayer is out of the country* for a continuous period of six months or more, the limitation period is suspended during his absence. The period of limitation does not expire until six months after he returns to the United States.

*Where property of a third party is wrongfully seized by the Government,* the limitation period is suspended. The suspension begins when the property is wrongfully seized or received and ends 30 days after the Treasury determines the levy was wrongful and returns the property. If the third party goes to court, the suspension ends 30 days after entry of a final judgment that the levy was wrongful.

## How You Consent to More Time for an IRS Examination

The expiration of statutory time in your case may be imminent at a time when the Agent has given little or no attention to your case. As a result, you may be asked to sign a waiver of the statute of limitations on a Form 872.

You may refuse to give your consent. What is the practical result of a refusal to consent?

*If you refuse before the Agent has had an opportunity to make an examination,* he can recommend the disallowance of every claimed deduction. A statutory notice of deficiency (90-day letter) can be sent on that basis. Since the refusal of an extension prevented any reasonable determination, he is forced to do this to protect the Government's interests. He can also recommend a jeopardy assessment. If a deficiency is issued without an audit, it may be attacked as being arbitrary.

If you refuse before the Agent has completed his examination or before he has time to consider the merits of your position, his recommendations will be based on the assumption that there is no merit in your position.

*If your refusal comes before the Group Chief or the Appeals Office* before either has an opportunity to consider the merits of your position, the Agent's recommendations might be sustained.

In all of these situations, the case may have to go to court. There will be delay and expenses. Consider these facts before you object to signing a Form 872.

You may stipulate on the Form 872 how long the statute of limitations is to be extended.

Form 872-A is used to extend the limitation period for cases under Appeals Office consideration. It permits flexibility by extending the limitation to a date 90 days after you are notified of a determination or 90 days after you terminate the agreement.

By agreeing to the extension, you can usually expedite a completion of the case by having requested data available as promptly as possible and by prodding gently but insistently for a final determination.

# PART TWO

PART TWO

# 7

# Treasury Audit Guides for Agents

The following pages present extracts from IRS audit guides suggesting techniques for examining tax returns. The guides are specifically prepared for agents preparing examinations of taxpayers' returns. The guides have been released to the public under the Freedom of Information Act.

A study of the extracts can help you prepare your case by giving you a perspective of the Agent's point of view and the questions he may ask about a particular issue.

## Background of Audits

The mission of the Internal Revenue Service is to encourage and achieve the highest possible degree of voluntary compliance with the tax laws and regulations and to maintain the highest possible degree of public confidence in the integrity and efficiency of the Service. The efficient examination of tax returns and the impartiality and integrity manifested by tax examiners serves as a means of accomplishing this objective.

The basic purpose of an income tax examination is to determine the correct tax liability of the person or entity whose return is being examined. In making the examination, the tax technician has a responsibility both to the taxpayer and the Government. Both parties, however, may be regarded as similar, in that neither is legally privileged to expect anything more than the proper determination of the tax liability.

## Taxpayer Relations Standards

Adequate time should be devoted to a discussion of the proposed adjustments to ensure that the taxpayer understands the adjustments.

Tact and discretion should be used to avoid discrediting an employee or representative of the taxpayer when pointing out errors in books and records or recommending disallowance of an unsubstantiated item.

Tax technicians should communicate the law to the taxpayer in terms that he will understand.

Tax technicians should advise the taxpayer of his rights of appeal, in all instances where there are indications of doubt or disagreement as to the application of the law.

Taxpayers should be educated as to requirements of the law with a view toward fostering voluntary compliance.

## General Taxpayer Relations

Good taxpayer relations are a necessary element to the success of any audit, and effective methods of handling interpersonal problems are no easy task. As expressed by the Commissioner, ". . . we may sometimes disagree with a taxpayer, but we should never be disagreeable. Our constant efforts to educate the public as to both their responsibilities and rights, together with a cooperative and understanding attitude on our side, will go a long way toward relieving the adversary climate which would otherwise prevail."

Each tax technician is not only an officer of the Government, but he is also a representative of the taxpayer. The responsibility of the Service is to determine and collect the correct tax. To fulfill his obligation to the taxpayer, the technician must ascertain that the tax is not overstated. Since the role of the tax technician is unique, he has a tremendous job in conducting himself in a manner which will inspire the cooperation and confidence of the taxpaying public.

To gain and keep the respect and voluntary cooperation of the taxpayer, the technician must have the proper "attitude" and acquire skills in how to deal with individual people. Attitude is a tendency or readiness for a person to act in a particular way. The requisite attitude for the technician is one of service to the taxpayer. Skill can be acquired through acceptance and application of the basic principles of taxpayer relations. However, lack of the appropriate attitude will negate the objective of improved taxpayer relations.

## Principles of Taxpayer Relations

*The goodwill and respect of the taxpayer can be won.* The tax technician must take a positive attitude in seeking ways to develop a favorable relationship with the taxpayer. People and their problems often appear to be more difficult than they are. Putting one's self in the taxpayer's place helps to understand him and his reactions.

*The first impression of a taxpayer is not always representative of the individual.* The behavior of people who act under the stress and disadvantage of incomplete information or misinformation is often not characteristic. Classifying people dogmatically should be avoided.

*The taxpayer's first impression of the people and procedures in the Internal Revenue Service is difficult to dislodge.* Oftentimes his first real contact with the Service is through Audit; consequently, it is necessary that the taxpayer does not receive an unfavorable impression of the Service when he makes his first contact.

*The appearance of a promise that should not have been made is as awkward as the promise itself.* Any effort to be helpful does not give license to mislead taxpayers to expect the impossible. A frank statement of the amount or extent of liability or of an action is much better than building up hopes that lead to an inevitable letdown.

*The dignity of the individual must always be respected and never violated.* Human beings have feelings and respond better when they are made to feel important instead of being belittled. Every taxpayer is important to the Internal Revenue Service.

*Each taxpayer tends to regard his situation as unique and one that requires special handling.* Routine matters that are handled graciously and pleasantly will give the taxpayer the impression that he is receiving special treatment.

*Inconvenience to the taxpayer should be reduced to a minimum.* Every effort should be made to provide a prompt solution to the taxpayer's problem, and reduce the number of actual contacts for him.

*Next to knowing is knowing where to find out quickly.* "I don't know," is an acceptable response to a taxpayer, provided it is followed by action which promptly gets the answer.

*A taxpayer in an office always considers himself more important than paper on someone's desk or in someone's hands.* He is generally right. If the paper is more important than the person, then those who work with the paper should be out of sight of the taxpayer.

*Patience is essential to the practice of being courteous.*

Being patient with an impatient person is a real test of one's ability to be courteous. Yet it is very important that patience be exercised in order to create a more favorable climate.

*The ability to explain smooths many difficult situations.* A good explanation is given patiently: starting from something the taxpayer surely knows, proceeding at a rate the taxpayer can follow, and concluding with a careful and understandable summary.

*A demonstration of anger can always be interpreted as inability to cope with the situation.* Even though some people are more difficult to deal with than others, a display of anger will almost always be interpreted as weakness. It does not promote a solution; it postpones one.

*Technical vocabulary to one person may be mere jargon to another.* To assume that the taxpayer is familiar with the technical terms of the Service may easily result in confusion and dissatisfaction.

## Nature of Taxpayer Contacts In Person

The philosophy of taxpayer contact operations and several general principles have been identified. Certain procedural pointers for the tax technician will further demonstrate the application of these principles and describe the nature of the personal contacts.

The taxpayer or his representative is a guest of the Internal Revenue Service, should be treated as one, and when he is so treated he will generally cooperate and try to be understanding.

Approach the taxpayer in a pleasant manner. A habit of signaling the taxpayer by a tilting of the head, by an arm motion, or by a crooking of the finger is not appropriate. When it is necessary for the taxpayer to wait, ask him to be seated and apologize for the delay.

Make the taxpayer feel that he is getting your undivided attention. Listen carefully, and formulate a plan for solving his problem as you listen. In matters of controversy, be polite but firm. Be certain of your point, and try to put it across without friction. When appropriate, show the taxpayer your authority for the position you are taking. When an error is found, if it is the taxpayer's, explain where and what it was and how it may be avoided in the future; if it is the Service's, admit it, and in a friendly way, despite the taxpayer's attitude, do all that can be done to correct it. If the error occurred in another branch or unit, do not criticize that source, for to do so does not improve that taxpayer's opinion of any part of the Service. Always assume that any error on the part of the Service has surely inconvenienced the taxpayer. It is not enough to apologize for "any inconvenience this may have caused" him. Apologize for the inconvenience it did cause him.

Avoid controversial subjects as well as unnecessary subjects. The taxpayer or his representative has a business or legal problem on his mind. There is no need to keep it simmering while the local ball teams, national weather changes, educational movements, or similar topics are introduced. If the taxpayer introduces a controversial subject, focus attention on his immediate problem and its solution.

Be alert to the possible development of offending mannerisms of speech. It is better to say, "You may be right," than to say, "That may be true," for the former questions neither one's honesty nor his facts. Grammatical errors and mispronunciations are just as noticeable as dirty hands or ungroomed hair to the taxpaying public. In addition, one neither commands by words nor summons with gestures when providing a service. A sign or a word that is intended to mean, "You may come over here now," can too easily be interpreted, "Come over here, you!"

When taxpayers are accompanied by other members of

the family, provide for the convenience of each one, if possible, regardless of age.

The taxpayer is looking for someone who is patient, fair, informed, and understanding. That person is you. Imagine yourself in the taxpayer's place. Try to understand his point of view; and you will more likely be that person the taxpayer is looking for.

## Nature of Taxpayer Contacts by Telephone

The objectives of professionalization of taxpayer contacts is very closely related to telephone conversations with the taxpayer or his representative. Although most of the calls are rather routine in nature, some are more difficult. It is true that most people find it easier to be sharp of tongue or bitter in expression when complaining to someone they cannot see. Some will yield to this temptation. There is never an excuse, however, for a representative of the Service to reply in kind.

As in personal contacts, there are additional procedural pointers for the tax technician that further demonstrate the application of the principles and describe the nature of telephone contacts. Most of these pointers are well expressed in recent training publications of telephone companies or in similar publications prepared for business or industrial use. A few of the specific points which reflect upon the nature of telephone contacts include:

Lift the receiver at the end of the first ring if possible.

When you do speak, do so for the purpose of starting and not postponing a conversation.

In answering the telephone, it is most effective to identify the function and to give your name.

If messages are taken for someone else, write them down at the time they are received.

In calling another person, give him time to answer.

When you expect your conversation to take some time, it is proper to ask the called person if he has a few minutes to talk about the particular subject.

It is better to say, "Would you mind giving me your name?" than "Who is calling, please?"

If it is necessary to leave the line to get information, unless the time will be very short, it is often better to offer to call the person back than to hold the line. Always make certain that the person has completed his instructions to you before leaving the line.

Thank people for waiting.

Handle calls to completion whenever it is practicable to do so.

If a call must be referred, refer it at the earliest opportunity so that the person calling will not have to repeat his whole problem.

Never hang up without giving a definite indication that the conversation is finished; "Goodbye" and "Thank you" are always acceptable.

Develop a pleasing telephone manner. Test your voice on friends until you know what your best telephone voice is, then practice it.

Avoid distorting facial expressions for they are often seen by other taxpayers that are present in the office.


## Nature of Taxpayer Contacts by Correspondence

Professionalization also applies to contacts through correspondence. As specific pointers have been listed for personal and for telephone contacts, so there are several pointers for specific application to correspondence contacts.

The taxpayer is as sensitive to misspelled words, poor grammar, stilted phrases, or poor typing, as are most people—for most people are taxpayers.

Form letters are always recognized as form letters by the taxpayer. If the form letter does not answer all the questions the taxpayer has raised, add additional sentences to cover the unanswered questions.

Taxpayers expect prompt replies and cannot understand any excuse for delay. Be prompt and the taxpayer feels you are giving his problem the attention it deserves.

Before sending a letter to a taxpayer, always reread it from the taxpayer's point of view. If it then appears awkward, inappropriate, or offensive, change it.

## Individual Returns—Forms 1040A

(Check) Dependents claimed, other than the taxpayer's own children, who had substantial income in relation to the stated amount provided by the taxpayer. For example, if the taxpayer claimed his parents as dependents and showed he provided $1,000 to each parent and each parent and others provided $900, there is a possibility that he has not considered nontaxable social security or other benefits. Such amounts when included in the support test might well offset the reported difference. If he claimed the parents or others besides his own children he may have failed to take into consideration the value of shelter which may have been furnished by another.

Small amount of income on a joint or single return with other dependents claimed. This may be an indication of unreported income or unallowable exemptions.

Claiming of an exemption for the spouse and indicating the spouse filed a return.

## Individual Returns—Forms 1040

(Check) Occupation which indicates probability of other income, such as tips, for waiters or waitresses, cab drivers, beauticians, porters, etc. Also occupations such as a fruit picker or crop harvester or similar seasonal workers may indicate the possibility of unreported off-season income. The possibility of unreported income is increased if the amount of income reported seems inadequate in view of the reported exemptions and deductions.

Joint return with signature of one spouse missing where the taxpayer claims the exemptions for both. The spouse may have filed separately claiming his or her own exemption.

Deductions or exclusions which are disproportionate in themselves or in relation to the taxpayer's occupation and indicated scope of duties or income, or which are estimated or inadequately explained. (Alimony, scholarship and fellowship grants, travel and entertainment, itemized deductions individually or in total, etc.)

Interest on home mortgage deducted but not property tax deducted, indicating the taxpayer may not be entitled to the interest deduction. Also, where a single person claims parents as dependents and these dependency deductions are questioned, there is a good possibility that the parents own the home. Further, it would generally be well to question any reported deduction for property taxes or interest concurrently.

Indications of possible omitted income, such as sale of stock during year but no dividends reported, installment sale of property but no interest reported, expenses reported under itemized deductions which relate to business income not reported, etc.

Stock losses or small gains on sale of stock in well-known companies which may be due to use of incorrect basis after stock dividends.

Sale of rental property at a loss where the facts indicate the property may have been the taxpayer's personal residence prior to conversion to rental purposes. Determine if correct basis is used. Also, if the facts indicate that the property was the taxpayer's personal residence on which no loss would be allowable. (Such items should be compared to the rent schedule.) Sale of business, bad debts, casualty losses, or other Schedule D transactions which are questionable under the circumstances. Also look for situations where the taxpayer may have applied the capital loss limitations on the sale of rental or other depreciable property.

Note the taxpayer's occupation. For example, if he is a carpenter, construction contractor, etc., he may have built or improved property rented or sold. He may have included the value of his own services and may have overstated the cost of materials by placing an estimated basis on the property in excess of cost. Any material used may have been obtained at reduced cost, or may have been charged to contract jobs. He may have furnished goods or services to others in return for goods or services. Any improvements or additions reported may be similarly overstated. If the date of acquisition compared to the amount of prior depreciation reported shows that the property may have been converted from a personal residence, it is possible that he built or made additions himself and overstated the basis.

## Married Taxpayers—Filing a Joint Return

Determine whether or not all income earned by both taxpayers has been included on the return. The tax auditor should specifically ask whether or not the other spouse had income. A wife may work for a short period of time, file separately for her refund, and also file a joint return with her husband.

Determine by direct questioning whether or not the taxpayers were actually married as of the last day of the taxable year.

Determine whether or not a common law marriage is involved and if so, whether or not it is recognized in the State where the taxpayer resided. Normally, this situation would be detected by information shown on the return or from questioning the taxpayer. The taxpayer may claim an exemption for a friend, boarder, companion, housekeeper, etc. The taxpayer may claim the joint return status without checking the status block or the exemption block for a spouse. The auditor should be alert to any statement made by the taxpayer which might indicate the existence of a common law marriage.

Determine whether or not either spouse was a nonresident alien at any time during the taxable year. Normally, this item would not be considered unless there is a specific reason for raising the issue, such as military personnel who may have married an alien during the year.

## Married Taxpayers—Filing Separately

Determine whether or not there is a duplicate claim for exemptions, nonbusiness deductions, credits, or duplicate reporting of income. When appropriate, the related return is secured by the auditor and inspected to determine whether or not there are any duplications.

Determine whether or not both husband and wife itemized deductions. The tax auditor should make an adjustment in a situation where one spouse itemized and the other did not.

## Unmarried Taxpayer—Head of Household

Determine whether or not a married person filing separately is claiming this status. The related returns should be compared to determine if this status is being claimed. In interview cases, the taxpayer may be able to advise whether his/her spouse is claiming this status or furnish a copy of the return.

Determine whether or not a taxpayer who is separated or divorced is claiming this status based on support of children who do not reside with him/her. A father may compute his tax on Head of Household rates and claim exemptions for children who do not reside with him. The auditor should ascertain whether or not the children being claimed resided with the taxpayer all year.

Determine whether or not the Head of Household rates should be denied as a result of a dependency disallowance. The auditor should be aware of the fact that the disallowance of a dependent may require an automatic denial of the use of the Head of Household rates. This occurs, for example, when a single woman is denied the exemption for her mother. It would then be necessary to disallow the use of the rates for Head of Household and compute the tax based on the rates for a single person.

Determine whether or not the exemption the taxpayer is claiming resulted from a multiple support agreement. The status of a return is not determined by a multiple support agreement. The taxpayer's father or mother must qualify as an allowable exemption and the taxpayer's unmarried child, grandchild, or step-child need not qualify as a dependent, providing other requirements as defined in section 2(b)(2) IRC are met, in order to claim the Head of Household status.

## Surviving Spouse With Dependent Child

Determine whether or not a surviving spouse without dependent children is erroneously claiming the rates applicable to a surviving spouse with children. Normally, this can be detected by an inspection of the return. This situation is generally more prevalent among elderly people since some fail to realize that they must properly claim dependent children before they may use the lower tax rates.

Determine the date of death. The auditor should ascertain the date of death and determine whether or not the return is for one of the two taxable years immediately following the close of the year in which the spouse died.

## Income—General

Auditors must be alert to detect the possibilities of omitted income. Some indications of possible unreported income may be apparent on the face of the return. In other cases the indications of possible omitted income may arise during the course of the examination.

It is well for auditors in interview cases to determine whether all income received during the year has been properly reported by asking the taxpayers if they received other income such as dividends, interest, etc. Taxpayers sometimes report wages subject to withholding but fail to report income from casual labor, piece work, contract work, domestic service, etc., upon which tax was not withheld.

The following describes some indications of unreported income which may be present on the return or arise during the examination:

The occupation line of the taxpayer may be indicative of unreported income. Waiters and waitresses, beauty operators, barbers, pullman porters, etc., may have unreported tip income.

Members of certain trades, such as plumbers, carpenters, and electricians may do part-time free lance work for homeowners and others.

Itinerants, such as fruit-pickers and seasonal workers,

may have income from other sources during the off-season.

Practical nurses may be employed by individuals as well as by hospitals or rest homes and the wages received from individuals may not be covered by a Form W-2.

Low income of one spouse may indicate the other spouse worked, possibly as domestic help or in another occupation, and the taxpayer may not have been furnished a Form W-2 or 1099.

A married taxpayer in certain community property States should report one-half the combined income of both spouses if a separate return is filed.

Income reported appears insufficient to meet the cost of living and other disbursements including those claimed on the return and possibly substantiated on audit, particularly when coupled with one of the above features.

Salespeople, union people and others who deduct business expenses may receive reimbursement for such expenses and sometimes an allowance for items of a non-deductible personal nature. They may indicate on the return that no reimbursement or allowance was received for the expenses by reasoning that the reimbursement or allowance received pertained to and equalled other expenses not shown per return and that the expenses deducted were not reimbursed. Any employee in an out-of-town travel status who does not include automobile expenses in business expense deductions should be questioned.

Executives of closely held corporations may receive money for personal expenses which are then classified on the corporate books as loans or advances, whereas it may actually represent additional compensation or dividends.

Direct questioning as to whether the spouse worked may reveal that he/she did but received less than the specified minimum amount of gross income and for that reason failed to report it.

Income reported from several employers should alert

the auditor to have the taxpayer account for the entire year's activities.

Reported stock transactions may indicate unreported dividends from the company. Auditors should ask taxpayers whether or not they received dividends, if none are reported.

Divorce cases indicate possible receipt of unreported alimony income.

Partnership income may be unreported. Development of expense deductions or gain or loss on the sale of assets may indicate the taxpayer was a member of a partnership during the year and may have income to report.

Reconciling reported partnership income with the reported distributive share shown on the partnership return for the year may reveal inaccurate reporting. Losses reported may be in excess of the partner's capital account in the partnership.

Development of information verifying reported deductions or income may reveal facts indicating the taxpayer is the beneficiary of an estate or trust and should have reported distributable income from that source.

Verification of rental schedules, depletion restoration cases, etc., may indicate that unreported rental income or royalties were received on other properties.

Salespeople and corporate executives are sometimes furnished company cars. Consideration should be given to the personal use of these cars. The fair market value of the personal usage is considered income.

Standardized pattern type letters may be used for making inquiry concerning certain types of unreported income, such as prizes and awards.

The reasons for failure to report the income should generally be developed and the file documented accordingly.

Unreported income in flagrant abuse cases may be the basis for referrals to intelligence and/or assertion of fraud or negligence penalties.

## Wages and Salaries

When examining taxpayers who earn income as employees, the auditor should be alert to recognize the relationship of the occupation line with other items which are or should be on the return. Examples of such interrelationships are:

Salesperson—This occupation when associated with the employer's name as shown on the return is often used to judge the allowability of expense deductions, and whether they should be deducted on page 1 or 2 of Form 1040. Examples of this are as follows:

A salesperson at a local retail store usually should not claim entertainment expense. This is particularly true with respect to a page 1 deduction.

An automobile salesperson's business expenses should usually appear only on page 2 (except for possible transportation expense). As many of these salespeople are furnished a car by their employer, the personal use element should be considered.

Milk or beer truck driver-salesperson or combination insurance collector-salesperson should not deduct business expenses other than for local transportation on page 1 of Form 1040.

Any salesperson in out-of-town travel status who does not include car expenses among business expenses should be asked why. If the car is furnished by the company, is there any personal use of it?

Members of certain trades usually work for contractors from whom they receive a W-2. Because of the nature of their work, they are apt to do part-time work for homeowners and others who are not likely to file W-2s. They should be directly questioned as to the possible existence of such income. Carpenters, painters, plumbers, electricians and the like are in this category.

The listing of a wife's occupation as housewife would

be inconsistent with a child care deduction. Of course, there could easily be a good explanation for this.

Auto mechanics showing deductions based upon the purchase of certain large items of equipment may have unreported income for part-time work for individual customers.

Bookkeepers and insurance brokers may also have unreported income from part-time assistance furnished taxpayers. They frequently have additional income from accounting and tax services rendered.

Additional techniques available for use where appropriate are as follows:

Ask the taxpayer if any Christmas or other bonus was received during the year and, if so, whether it was included in the Form W-2. If the taxpayer did receive such a bonus and does not know if it was so included, ask him/her to secure this information from the employer.

If the taxpayer's occupation is such that he/she was employed by a number of different employers during the year, so that there were several W-2's, it is possible that one or more W-2's were not listed on the tax return. This is particularly true of construction workers, itinerant workers and the like. In these cases, it is wise to have the taxpayer account for employment chronologically throughout the year. The taxpayer should be requested to produce retained W-2 copies as in some cases the originals are removed from the filed Form 1040 before the auditor receives it. The retained copies might also include W-2's which the taxpayer did not list on the return because they had not been received at the time the return was filed.

## Tips

Returns of taxpayers reporting income from occupations where tips are commonly received should be carefully reviewed to determine if all income was reported.

Taxpayers who receive tip income may not maintain complete and accurate records. The auditor should therefore determine whether the amounts reported are correct. Some taxpayers report relatively small amounts of tip income while others may not report any. Since this is an area where flagrant abuses of unreported or understated income may exist, the examiner should adopt a vigorous approach to the problem. Future voluntary compliance on the part of a taxpayer receiving tip income will depend to a great extent on the manner in which this problem is handled in the current year.

The following are some techniques which should aid the tax auditor when verifying tip income, particularly where adequate records are lacking or there is serious doubt as to accuracy of those records that are kept.

Application of Certain Percentage to Table Sales per Waiter-hour to Determine Tip Income per Waiter hour. This method would normally be used in a situation where a tip project has been undertaken. The return of a particular hotel or restaurant will be examined, and selected information will be obtained and passed on to Office Audit. Two examples of this type of situation follow.

1. Assume that all sales in a particular restaurant were made by waitresses. The Revenue Agent who examined the restaurant's return furnished the names of the waitresses and the total sales made by each. A previously determined percentage can then be applied to the sales made by each waitress. If a particular waitress made $10,000 in sales and a percentage of 10 percent was applied against this figure, her tip income would be $1,000.

2. Assume the Revenue Agent determined that the restaurant had one million dollars in sales made by waitresses during the year. The Revenue Agent also checked the payroll records and determined the total number of hours worked by all waitresses to determine the average hourly tip income. The hourly tip income would then be multi-

plied by the total hours worked by each waitress to arrive at her tip income. For example, assume that a particular waitress worked 1,600 hours during the year and the total sales made by all waitresses was one million dollars. Ten percent of this figure, $100,000, representing tip income, is then divided by 105,000 hours which is the total hours worked by all waitresses. The result is .952 dollars ($.952) per hour which is then multiplied by the 1,600 hours worked by the taxpayer. The answer is $1,524.20 which is the tip income the taxpayer should have reported. While the examples used 10 percent, it should be noted that this percentage varies according to type and class of establishment as well as other factors.

Busboys, maitre d's, etc., usually receive fairly set amounts from each waiter (waitress) per shift. Their tips thus can be computed on a per shift basis.

Taxi Drivers Tips—Cab drivers' tips may be established by applying a certain percent to their bookings or readings. Their employers may show these bookings on their W-2's. If they do not but the drivers' salaries are a percentage of bookings, tip income can be determined by working backward from the W-2 and reconstructing the bookings as in the following example.

| | |
|---|---|
| Salary per W-2 | $1,750 |
| Percentage of bookings which is paid as salary | 35% |
| Bookings as reconstructed (100/35 x $1,750) | $5,000 |
| Estimated tip income, 10% thereof | $ 500 |

In examining the returns of taxi drivers, the auditor should determine whether the cab fare is based on meter rates (time and distance) or on a zone basis.

Beauticians usually receive a percentage of the total charge (such as 40% or 60%) with a minimum guarantee. Their gross receipts can be reconstructed and a tip percentage applied in a manner similar to the method used for taxi drivers.

Use of a Set Percentage Which Represents the Charge to the Customer Made by the Hotel or Restaurant to Provide for Tips at a Banquet or Catered Affair—This method can normally be employed in a situation where the taxpayer receives most of his/her tips for services performed at a banquet or catered affair. In this situation, a predetermined tip fee is added to the fixed charge by the hotel or restaurant for a banquet or catered affair. The total tip income is then divided among the waiters and/or waitresses who service the affair. If a taxpayer failed to maintain adequate records and this information is not available from the employer, the auditor may desire to reconstruct the tip income by obtaining information from both the employer and the employee in relation to the average tip income per banquet and the number of banquets serviced by the taxpayer.

Comparison of Tip Income Reported by Other Tip Recipients Similarly Employed—In ascertaining whether a particular taxpayer has reported the correct amount of tip income, the auditor might compare tip income reported by other tip recipients under similar circumstances in the same area. This comparison should be used as a guide only and would be but one of several factors the auditor should consider.

Determination as to Whether Pooled Tip Income is Involved—Some restaurants maintain a system whereby all tip income received by personnel performing services is pooled and divided equally among them. The control and operation of this system may be vested with the cashier, head waiter, etc., or with the management. Under this system, records are normally maintained, and each member of the "pool" is informed of the tip income received on a daily, weekly, monthly, or annual basis. The auditor should request the taxpayer to present this statement and/or statements for the purpose of comparing the figure thereon with the figure on the return. An example of this would be a situation where 10 waiters pool all tips received. If the total tip income in the pool for a particular day was $200, this amount would be divided by 10, and each waiter would receive $20 as his share of the tip income. There may be variations of this system but the principle remains the same, and the taxpayer should have or be able to obtain accurate records of the tip income received.

It is recognized that the reconstruction of unreported tip income where records are inadequate is a difficult and sensitive area. However, this should not deter the examiner in an endeavor to determine the correct amount of tax liability. Whether any penalties are asserted would normally depend on the facts and circumstances of each case including the degree of noncompliance, amount involved, cooperation extended by the taxpayer, and records maintained by the taxpayer.

## Dividends

The audit of dividend income reported by the taxpayer should not be limited to the information documents attached to the return. If more than $100 is excluded, the ownership of securities by both husband and wife should be ascertained.

In interview audits, the auditors should analyze the method used by the taxpayer in determining his/her dividend income. Understanding the method used may suggest the most appropriate way to check for accuracy. A list of securities owned at the beginning of the taxable year, used in conjunction with subsequent sales and acquisitions, will afford the most exact results.

If the taxpayer merely records dividends when received and also keeps some securities in the broker's custody, the broker's monthly statements should be checked carefully for dividends credited to the account. Most taxpayers who have any security trades during the year retain their monthly statements. These statements should be checked when verifying dividend income.

Information regarding dividend payments by publicly held corporations is available from many sources in Audit Division libraries. Financial publications issued annually included Moody's, Poor's, and Fitch's Dividend Services.

Farmers' cooperative dividends may be reported in one or two ways on a return; as dividend income or as a reduction of purchases. Farmers' returns should be examined carefully to see that they are reported.

Distributions by corporations, which are in whole or in part nontaxable, are tabulated in various services such as Prentice-Hall and Commerce Clearing House Capital Adjustment Services. Nontaxable dividends must be approved by the Internal Revenue Service even though they may be listed in these Services. Corporations whose distributions most commonly have irregular features include railroads, mining companies, investment companies, mutual funds, and utility companies.

The following general rules apply for reporting dividends on stock sold:

When stock is sold and a dividend is both declared and paid after the date of sale, such dividend is not income to the seller.

When stock is sold after the declaration of a dividend and after the date the seller is entitled to the dividend, it ordinarily is income to the seller.

When stock is sold between the date of declaration and the date of payment of dividend and the sale takes place at such time that the purchaser becomes entitled to the dividend, the dividend ordinarily is income to the buyer.

Standard questionnaires are provided for this issue, and may prove useful in some interview cases when enclosed with the appointment letter. The questionnaires, when properly executed, facilitate file documentation, and can be used as a guide to auditors during interviews.

Ascertain that proper distinction is made between dividend income from domestic and foreign corporations and interest income. This is especially significant since each type of income may be subject to its own specific exclusion.

Savings and Loan interest as well as Credit Union interest, though commonly called dividends, are treated as interest income for tax purposes.

## Interest

The verification of interest income should also be made in conjunction with the audit of capital transactions. Interest bearing securities sold during the year should be compared to interest reported. The interest accrued to date of sale is sometimes reported as part of the proceeds, rather than as interest income.

If the taxpayer maintains brokerage accounts, the statements should be analyzed. Interest charged on margin accounts may not be netted against interest or dividend income. It must be claimed as an itemized deduction. In the analysis, make sure that no deduction has been claimed for interest paid to carry tax-exempt securities.

Taxpayers should always be asked whether they have cashed any Government bonds, held any matured Government bonds, or had any savings accounts during the taxable year. Some States require that the individual have an account as a prerequisite to leasing a safe deposit box in a savings bank. If a deduction for the box rental is claimed in such cases, a savings account is indicated. Similarly, if the taxpayer uses savings bank money orders or cashier's checks to substantiate deductions, inquiry should be directed to a savings account.

Other interest income items often erroneously omitted from returns include interest on paid up insurance policies, interest on prior year tax refunds, interest on G.I. insurance dividends on deposit with the Veterans Administration, and interest on insurance dividends on deposit with an insurance company which are withdrawable upon demand and taxable to the policyholder, when credited to his/her account.

If property was sold in prior or current years and a purchase money mortgage or second mortgage constituted part payment, interest income should be reflected in the return. A common error is to regard all mortgage collections as principal until it is fully paid.

Taxpayers sometimes transfer ownership in outstanding Series E Bonds. When this is done, interest income earned on such bonds must be reported in the year of transfer.

Where it is claimed that interest income is either fully or partially tax exempt, or nontaxable, determine the propriety thereof (State or municipal bonds; certain Government bonds acquired prior to March 1, 1964; distributions representing partial return of capital, etc.)

Interest received on a condemnation award is very often included as part of the capital gain instead of ordinary income.

## Rentals

Usually the audit of a single rental return is accomplished by correspondence. However, an interview may be necessary for those returns reflecting multi-unit property, more than one piece of rental property, and conversion from a personal residence to rental property.

The following points should be considered whether or not the rental property is occupied by taxpayer:

Question taxpayer directly about the weekly or monthly rent received for each unit and periods of vacancy, if any.

Where rents are received in advance on either the cash or the accrual basis and there is no substantial limitation on their disposition, they constitute taxable income when received (constructive receipt).

A bonus paid by the lessee to the lessor upon execution of the lease constitutes income. Similarly, so is a lump sum amount paid by the lessee in consideration for the cancellation of a lease.

The performance of services by a tenant in lieu of rental payments constitutes income. Such may be detected where the value of such services is claimed as an expense.

Examine the purchase contract to determine if land is being depreciated. This error is common in returns of small taxpayers. If the purchase contract is not available, reference can be made to the real estate tax assessments for the year of acquisition.

Proper application of the depreciation "allowed or allowable" rules is often not made in small taxpayer returns. To determine this, it may be necessary in some cases to check retained copies of prior years income tax returns.

Where the taxpayer presents a property management statement as support for the items reported, the underlying paid bills should be requested. Classification of expenses on such statements is often poor, particularly with respect to capital items.

Property management fees in excess of the customary amount paid for such services to independent management concerns should receive particular attention. Where this rate is exceeded, the possibility exists that the payment is other than a business expense. It is one way of supporting an aged parent or of making a gift to a child or other relative.

The provisions of section 164(d) IRC regarding real estate tax apportionment should be considered where the rental property was acquired during the taxable year (or the immediately preceding year in some States). The sales agreement often shows a proration of property taxes whereby the purchaser has reimbursed the seller for taxes previously paid.

Has a casualty loss for windstorm, flood, or other damage been allowed which would decrease the basis?

The following points should be considered where the taxpayer occupies the property:

Auditors should determine that expenses are properly grouped as to tenant only, taxpayer only, and common to both.

That portion of depreciation, repairs, and other expenses attributable to the taxpayer's living quarters should be segregated from the totals of such expenses. At times the taxpayer will allocate such expenses. However, the auditor should make sure that all expenses on the property have been reallocated between the business and personal portions.

Real estate taxes and interest should be properly apportioned between itemized deductions and rental expense.

In a loss situation, look for fictitious rental income for taxpayer's occupancy with all expenses then becoming deductible without apportionment.

Allowance should be made for variance of apartment sizes. For example, there may be a three-room and a six-room apartment in one rental unit. Apportionment should not be made on a 50-50 basis, but rather on the basis of available occupancy space. Personal occupancy of 800 square feet by a taxpayer of a 2,400 square foot property would result in a 66⅔ percent (1,600 + 2,400) business apportionment.

A net loss from rentals is sometimes attributable to the fact that the property is rented to a relative or friend for an amount less than the rental value of the property. In such a case, the loss is usually not deductible.

## Royalties

The royalty contract should be scrutinized to determine that the taxpayer has an economic interest. If the taxpayer gives up all rights in the property from which income is derived, the amounts received are considered payments for the sale or exchange of the property rather than royalty income.

It is not uncommon, however, for taxpayers to report royalty income as a capital gain. The terms of the contract must be scrutinized to determine whether the taxpayer has sold the property, i.e. divested himself/herself of his/her rights, title and interest, or granted a franchise or right for use only, resulting in ordinary income.

Royalties received from copyrights or patents are usually paid on a unit basis, such as, number of books, machines, tickets sold, etc.

Taxpayers sometimes deduct research and development costs of patents or copyrights as expenses when they should be capitalized. Expenses of writing a book is an example. However, when such costs are incurred after the book has been published, they are deductible as expenses. Where patent royalties are concerned, the usual deduction is the amortization of the taxpayer's capital cost of the patent.

When a patent becomes valueless before its expiration, the unrecovered cost or other basis is deductible in that year. Taxpayers should be able to furnish documentary evidence of worthlessness by third-party statements.

Depletion is allowable to the owner of an economic interest in property of mineral deposits, oil, gas, or timber. It provides for the recovery of costs over the economic life of the property.

When checking the depletion deduction, be certain that the adjusted basis of the property has been properly computed.

Where percentage depletion has been used, ascertain that the proper rates of depletion and the statutory limitations have been complied with.

Depletion for timber occurs when the timber is cut and the deduction should be taken in the year of sale, even though the latter may occur years after the cutting process. Timber is cut when in the ordinary course of business the quantity of felled timber is determined, whether it is cut by the taxpayer or under contract with others.

Depletable assets differ from other assets for tax purposes, and they are regarded as being owned by the beneficial or equitable owners rather than by owners of title. For example, the fee owner of land conveys a lease to an operator in return for a ⅛ interest in any oil production. The operator then sells equally to each of six investors ⅚ of his/her ⅞ interest. The legal title to the land is still held by the original owner but equitable title, or the economic interest is held ⅛ each by the legal owner, the operator, and the six investors.

Where royalties are received in advance on either the cash or the accrual basis and there is no substantial limitation on their disposition, they constitute income when received.

When royalties are paid by the producing company, the taxpayer has no expenses directly related to the production of the income except the allowable depletion. Sometimes taxpayers improperly deduct travel and other expenses. Statements are issued by the producing companies setting forth royalties subject to depletion and should be requested.

Taxpayers who receive royalty income may fail to restore bonus depletion as required if the lease is terminated without production. Failure to renew the lease or failure to pay rentals may terminate the lease.

When examining returns reporting royalty income, inquiry should be made concerning existence of other leases to determine whether rentals or bonuses were received or a lease terminated resulting in the restoration of a bonus depletion.

## Employer-Employee Financed Plans

The Code distinguishes between employer-employee financed annuities, where the employee's cost will be recovered within three years and between other so-called general rule annuities.

The cost of an annuity may be established by a statement from the employer or insurance company as the case may be. If there is no insurance company statement, it may be necessary to determine cost from the annuity contract. This contract should set forth the total consideration paid for the annuity whether as a lump sum or as periodic payments over a given period. Where employee annuities are involved, the statement from the employer or the insurance company should clearly indicate that portion of the cost which was contributed by the employee. Any interest earned on funds of an annuity are not to be considered as part of the cost of the annuity.

If the taxpayer is the beneficiary of a deceased employee and receives a pension or annuity which qualified for a death benefit exclusion to $5,000, the exclusion is to be added to the unrecovered cost of the annuity in calculating, at the annuity starting date, the investment in the contract. The death benefit exclusion is not applicable if the deceased employee had received any retirement pension or annuity payment under a joint and survivorship contract after reaching his/her retirement age.

## Prizes and Awards

Returns involving unreported prizes or awards will usually have newspaper clippings, information reports, or other evidence attached for the auditor's scrutiny.

Where, after contact with the taxpayer the auditor has no indication of the fair market value of the article or service received, the auditor may have to resort to a third party, such as the company awarding the prize, or make collateral requests. The time for determining the fair market value of the article is the date received by the taxpayer. Valuations made after the date the article was received and presented to the taxpayer are immaterial.

Salespersons sometimes receive and fail to report expense-paid trips for exceeding sales quotas. The usual contention is that it was a business trip. However, by obtaining a statement from the employer, or determining percentage of time devoted to various activities and reviewing the trip brochure, the auditor should be able to ascertain the purpose of the trip.

## Gains and Losses From Sale or Exchange of Property

The technique to be used in the audit of the gains and losses reported on a return will usually vary depending on the nature of the asset. The two broad classifications of assets, both under the law and for purposes of audit approach, are capital assets and all other assets.

Capital assets—The verification of gains and losses involves several elements: the selling price, expenses of sale, the adjusted basis of the property, and the holding period.

The most common capital transactions appearing on nonbusiness returns are sales of securities. Normally they are effected through brokers if they are listed securities. When such is the case, the brokerage "bought" and "sold" slips and the broker's monthly statements are the best approach to this phase of an examination. The transaction slips state the purchase price or sales price, the commissions, the transfer taxes (Federal and local), and accrued interest where appropriate. In addition, the dates of the transaction are clearly set forth.

Verification of capital transactions from brokers' slips and statements should be made in conjunction with auditing of dividend and interest income. This dual check can indicate both errors in the dividend and interest reported and also omitted transactions.

If the capital transactions reported were not made through a broker, the proceeds and expenses of sale should receive closer scrutiny. Disposition of securities in a closely held corporation should be checked as to the valuation of property received, when in a form other than cash. This valuation should be based on fair market value. A common error is the reporting of gain or loss based on the surplus or deficit.

Holding period—Because the Code varies its treatment of gains or losses depending upon the holding period of the capital asset, the dates of acquisition and disposal are important. They are also important in connection with losses arising out of wash sales and in cases of property acquired in a tax-free exchange. See section 1223 IRC pertaining to holding period in such cases. The general rule for determining the holding period is that such period begins the day after contractual purchase (regardless of later delivery or payment date) and ends on the day of contractual sale. Therefore in verifying sales on a security exchange the contract date, not the settlement date, is governing. Further refinements have been made by the Service. In the case of a cash basis taxpayer, the loss on a transaction is deemed to have been realized upon the date of sale despite the fact that the proceeds were received in a subsequent taxable year.

Expense of sale—Capital transactions are rarely reported in which there is no appropriate expense of sale. These expenses include legal, accounting and brokerage fees. When gains or losses appear on a return and no such expenses are set out, the auditor should determine that they have not been claimed as ordinary deductions. Frequently these expenses are netted against the selling price which is satisfactory.

Personal residence—Because the Code provides unique treatment with respect to gains on the sale or exchange of a residence, Form 2119 is a useful worksheet to use in beginning the audit of such gain.

When the information is not available from the return and the taxpayer is claiming nonrecognition of all or part of the gain, he/she should be asked to complete Form 2119. In many cases, it will be necessary to use facts stemming from years other than the one under examination. This is true because of the latitude of time provided in the Code for replacement or reinvestment. It is important for the auditor to realize that completion of the form by the taxpayer is not the equivalent of auditing the transaction. The amounts entered on the form must be verified.

As in the case of any real property, the settlement statement is the best approach to checking the transaction. Where at all possible, the taxpayer should be requested to submit the purchase and sale statements.

Where the property was inherited, determination of the correct basis may be done by an inspection of copies of the estate tax return or appraisal statements. Where it was received as a gift, inspection may be made of the gift tax return. The taxpayer may have copies of these returns.

In addition to the purchase price, the taxpayer usually claims capital additions in the adjusted basis. Unlike the case of rental property, no deductions are allowable for repairs to a residence. Therefore, when reporting rental income, the taxpayer's normal inclination is to shade his/her judgment in favor of expense over capital charge. On the other hand, in reporting the sale of a residence, the inclination is to regard all prior repairs and expenses as capital additions. To verify the taxpayer's claim for such improvements during the holding period, the tax auditor must clearly understand the distinction between expense and capital items.

Receipted bills of contractors who performed the work would be useful. Comparison of the amount shown on such a bill should be made with the amount of disbursement. The inspection of a canceled check, for instance, may reveal that the amount of the bill was reduced because of protest by the taxpayer.

The building codes in most communities require the filing of plans before permits are issued for making material renovations and additions. This evidence should be requested if the auditor has no other means of determining the facts.

When the sale of a residence is reported, and it was acquired after 1949, particular attention should be given the adjusted basis. It is necessary to determine whether the adjusted basis property reflects any nonrecognized gain realized from a prior sale. In computing the cost of a residence and the capital improvements, an analysis should be made to determine that the value of the taxpayer's labor is not included. In addition, casualty losses previously allowed are a reduction of the basis whereas appropriate reconstruction after the casualty is an addition to the cost.

Multiple dwellings—Frequently property is sold which consists in part of the taxpayer's residence. The approach to verifying such transactions should take the form of dividing the sale into two parts, one for the residence, the other for the rental property. Treating the sale in two parts often results in a nonallowable loss on the residence portion and a taxable gain on the rental portion.

In dividing the sale transaction, proper allocation must be made for original cost and capital additions between the personal and rental portions of the asset. All depreciation allowed or allowable is an adjustment to the basis of the rental portion only. Similarly, the selling price and expenses of sale must also be allocated between the two segments. The separate gain or loss is measured for each segment, personal and rental, and proper tax treatment applied to each. Regarding the sale as a single transaction allows the taxpayer to offset a nondeductible loss against a taxable gain.

Various methods are available for allocating costs and selling prices between the personal and rental portions. One acceptable method is the ratio of rental value of the two segments. The allocation of capital additions between the personal and rental parts must be tempered by the taxpayer's normal inclination to spend more money on his/ her own residence. This should be taken into account absent reasonable substantiation for prorating the costs.

The sale of property that is part personal and part rental, if held more than one year will be treated as a section 1231 transaction for the rental portion. This portion should be verified in the same manner as though it were an independent sale of property held solely for rental income. The check is similar to that involved in the sale of business property.

The business or personal use of a dwelling may also be temporary or sporadic. An example is a residence in a resort area, or part of which is occasionally used for production of rental income.

Appraisal statements are usually acceptable for verifying the basis of property, especially where personal property or portions thereof have been converted to rental use. These statements should be made by a qualified appraiser and show a logical and acceptable basis for fixing the probable value at the date the property was received or converted. Such appraisals are sometimes a basis for making an FHA loan.

Installment sales—The tax auditor must be thoroughly familiar with the installment sales provisions of the Code and regulations and be certain that all requirements are met. The common errors are for taxpayers to improperly compute the amount realized in the year of sale, or payments on the principal or the percentage of gross profit for the year. Very often the taxpayer received interest income which was not reported. When auditing installment sales, determine whether the taxpayer has properly included:

Payments in the taxable year other than the initial payment;

Earnest money deposit or option payments;

Any accrued interest, taxes, or other liabilities of the taxpayer paid by the purchaser;

Any mortgage paid off for the taxpayer by the buyer;

Any mortgage assumed by the purchaser over the taxpayer's adjusted basis in the property;

Any notes receivable from third parties or other property given the taxpayer;

Noncash down payments, i.e. a trailer, house, car, etc. turned over to the seller;

Capital loss carryover—When a taxpayer has a capital loss carryover, the computation of the loss in the year in which it arose and the computation of income for any other year to which the loss should have been carried is subject to verification.

Often the sale of noncapital assets is included in the loss computation because taxpayers failed to properly classify the assets sold.

Where the loss year and/or the intervening years have not been examined, the taxpayer's retained copies of the returns should be inspected. If the taxpayer fails to produce retained copies the auditor should consult the group manager to determine whether to secure the original returns.

Ordinary income vs. capital gains—in determining whether income from the sale of assets should be taxed as ordinary income rather than as capital gains, the tax auditor should look for:

Sales of depreciable property to related taxpayers;
Dealings in a manner which would constitute a trade or business, i.e. subdivision of a tract of land and sale of its lots upon which substantial improvements have been made;
Redemption of stock by a closely held corporation;
Dealings with related individuals (substance vs. form).

## Scholarship and Fellowship Grants

When examining this issue the following questions should be answered:

Is the grantor a tax-exempt organization, or a government unit or agency?

What is the purpose of the grant, the period of the grant, and for whose primary benefit is the grant?

What portion, if any, of the reported grant, constitutes compensation for services rendered or to be rendered?

Is reimbursement for travel and other expenses specifically stated in the grant?

Has the limitation been applied to the amount excludable from income where the recipient is not a candidate for a degree?

Some grantors issue their own publications wherein they indicate the tax consequences to the recipients. However, such statements by the grantor should be viewed only as their opinion. The auditor should be certain that the taxpayer has complied fully with the provisions of section 117 IRC.

Recipients who are candidates for a degree often receive part of the scholarship or fellowship grant, compensation for teaching, research, or other services in the nature of part-time employment which is required as a condition to receiving the scholarship or fellowship grant. As an example, a graduate student studying for his Ph.D. in English received an award as a "teaching fellow," a requirement being that he conduct three classes per week for freshmen English students. To determine excludability, the auditor should ascertain whether all candidates for the same degree are required to perform similar services.

## Earned Income From Sources Without the United States

There are four basic elements which should be verified when auditing this issue:

1. Determine if the exclusion is claimed as a bona fide resident or for physical presence in a foreign country;
2. Ascertain that the time requirements have been met;
3. Ascertain that the excluded income qualifies as earned income;
4. Ascertain that no deductions are claimed which are attributable to the excluded income.

Residence abroad—In order to determine item (1) above, the tax auditor should secure such information as the name of the foreign country and the employer's name. If the taxpayer returned to the United States, find out the reason; e.g. vacation, resignation, completion of work abroad, or temporary assignment in the United States in connection with the job in the foreign country.

Activity in domestic life of foreign country—To further determine item (1) above, ascertain the type of visa secured for entry into the foreign country: whether the taxpayer has applied for foreign citizenship; whether the taxpayer is required to pay foreign income taxes; address in foreign country; type of dwelling resided in (i.e. purchased home, hotel or other rented quarters, company furnished quarters); address where family resided; local foreign schools attended by taxpayer's children; and citizenship of children and spouse.

Employment abroad—in connection with item (2) above, the following information would be helpful: name of employer; nature of work performed, and basis of employment, i.e. permanent, for an indefinite period, length of contract, whether or not there is an option to extend the term; and, whether or not taxpayer will return to the United States at the completion of a project. When determining item (3) above, ascertain types of income received by taxpayer, such as salary or wages, commissions or fees, etc.

## Foreign Tax Credit

Generally, income, war-profits, and excess-profits taxes paid or accrued during the tax year to any foreign country or U.S. possession may be taken as a credit or a deduction against the Federal tax. To do this, an individual must submit with his/her return, a Form 1116 (Statement in Support of Credit Claimed by an Individual or Fiduciary for Taxes Paid or Accrued to Foreign Countries or Possessions of the United States).

A foreign tax credit or deduction claimed is an immediate flag to the tax auditor that income from foreign sources should also be reflected on the return. Where all foreign income is exempt from gross income no credit or deduction for foreign taxes is allowable.

In order to claim the credit or the deduction, the taxpayer must itemize his/her deductions.

It is usually to the individual's advantage to take the tax as a deduction when he/she has a negative taxable income (e.g., net operating loss).

## Net Operating Loss Deduction

Occasionally, on a nonbusiness return, a net operating loss deduction will appear, due to the fact that the taxpayer is no longer in business or due to the fact that the taxpayer belongs to a partnership or is a stockholder in a small business corporation, or because the net operating loss arose from a casualty loss. In each of these cases, the computation of the loss in the year in which it arose and computation of income for any other year to which the loss should have been carried, is subject to verification. The income in a closed year may be adjusted and reflected in the NOL carryback and carryover even though any resulting increase in tax liability cannot be assessed for the closed year.

## Casualty and Theft Losses

Casualty losses affecting items incidental to real property, such as trees or shrubbery, must be verified as a loss of a minor portion of the asset. The shrinkage in market value, limited to adjusted basis, which forms the allowable deduction, must be determined by reference to the property as a whole, both as to fair market value and adjusted basis.

Theft losses are deductible only in the year of discovery. In the verification of the deductible loss resulting from the theft, the tax auditor should determine that a theft in fact did occur. Since it is common practice to report a theft to the police authorities, the nonexistence of such a report could be material and might lead to the determination that the property was merely displaced or lost and that, therefore, no deduction is allowable.

# Traveling and Entertainment Expenses—General

Many audit techniques for verifying travel and entertainment deductions are common to both the nonbusiness and the business return. For this reason audit techniques for travel and entertainment deductions discussed in this section are applicable to the employee as well as the self-employed individual.

If the return does not include a schedule of expenses, the tax auditor should have the taxpayer complete Form 2106 (Statement of Employee Business Expenses).

It is the employer who is expected to define the range of the employee's business. Outside salespersons who incur entertainment expense are exceptions to this rule because they are more in the nature of independent contractors since the amount of income is dependent upon sales.

The taxpayer's occupation can be an aid in determining whether or not he/she is reimbursed. Often salaried persons are reimbursed by their employers for certain expenses incurred in carrying on the employer's business. If there is any question as to the amount of the reimbursement or as to the fact that the taxpayer was obligated to incur expenses, the auditor should ask the taxpayer to secure a letter from his/her employer. It is not sufficient that the letter merely states that the employee is obligated to travel in the interest of the employer. The tax auditor should insist on the letter containing a positive statement as to whether the employee was reimbursed and, if so, how much and whether the amount is included in the Form W-2. Such a letter would be of doubtful value if the employer is a corporation in which the taxpayer is the principal stockholder or if the employer is related to the employee.

Once the question of reimbursement has been determined, the taxpayer's deduction must be substantiated.

## Travel Away From Home

From the standpoint of audit techniques the tax auditor should consider asking the following questions:

Name and location of employer?

City where hired and date?

Location of job and inclusive dates of employment?

How long did the taxpayer expect to be there at the outset? Why?

Any change in expectation thereafter? Why?

Where was the taxpayer's family living?

Where was the taxpayer living?

Company facilities or transportation provided and if not used, why?

Name and address of local union to which the taxpayer belonged, and length of membership?

Permanent residence address, if any? Why? How long? Is it owned?

Where did the taxpayer live between jobs and why?

Work history. Where is the taxpayer usually employed? When was he/she last employed there? For how long?

Expenses incurred?

Reimbursement or allowance received?

## Local Travel

While the regulations refer to traveling "away from home," the recordkeeping requirements of the regulations are still applicable for local travel. The tax auditor will encounter situations of local travel where, for instance, a salesperson has accounts within a metropolitan area.

The Cohan Rule—In local travel cases where there is a minimum of substantiation as to amount and business purpose, the so-called Cohan rule is applicable. George M. Cohan was a well-known playwright and actor. A lower court sustained the Commissioner in disallowing his entire claimed deduction for travel (and entertainment) expenses. This decision was reversed by the higher court which pointed out that since there had been an admission by the lower court that some monies were spent, and that these monies would have been deductible if supported, the lack of any detailed accounting for the monies was not sufficient reason for disallowing the deduction in full. It charged the lower court to make as close an approximation as possible, bearing heavily against the taxpayer since the entire proceedings were caused by his own inexactitude.

Some taxpayers may feel that they need only claim that monies were spent for travel and without any further substantiation the Cohan rule will apply. In so doing they may ignore the three requisites established in the Cohan case and later cases which permit an approximation. They are:

1. That the expense claimed is so directly related to the business of the taxpayer that it qualifies as an ordinary and necessary business expense;
2. That some expense was actually incurred; and
3. That a basis for approximation has been constructed from available evidence both as to amount and business purpose of the expenditure claimed.

When using the Cohan rule, the tax auditor must insist that the taxpayer meet the above requisites. Further, in those cases where the approximation is a recurring adjustment, consideration should be given to making the "bearing heavily" progressively onerous on the taxpayer.

The auditor's report in a follow-up examination should state whether and to what extent the taxpayer has corrected the inadequacies of recordkeeping.

In some cases the taxpayer's principal record of travel expenses is a diary. If this information in the diary is kept concurrently and sufficient detail to enable the auditor to identify the amounts and nature of the expenditures, such records may be considered adequate, even though most of the daily entries are not supported by receipted bills or cancelled checks. However, where the total amount of such expenses appears to be disproportionate to the taxpayer's income and business activities, the taxpayer should be required to corroborate the book entries by furnishing documentary proof or collateral evidence.

Checks paid to credit card systems are, in themselves, inadequate substantiation of deductions claimed. The taxpayer must also maintain a record of the business nature of the expenditures.

Checks paid to "Cash" are not considered adequate substantiation unless the taxpayer maintains adequate records on the nature of his/her expenditures.

It is important to note that the doctrine of the Cohan case has been superseded to the extent of travel away from home and entertainment and is not applicable only in instances of local travel.

## Automobile Expenses

The taxpayer may claim the cost of operating an automobile for travel away from home and local travel.

Where taxpayers elect to use the standard mileage rates, they must establish their business mileage for local transportation and for travel away from home.

A taxpayer may use the standard mileage rate irrespective of whether a reimbursement or allowance for such business automobile expense was received from his/her employer, provided such reimbursement or allowance is reported.

Where the taxpayer does not use these standard mileage rates, he/she must compute the cost of operations, based on actual expenses and depreciation for local travel and travel away from home.

In determining auto business mileage, a suggested approach is to first verify total mileage and then determine business mileage or personal mileage, whichever is easier based on the facts and circumstances. Once these figures are established, expenses can be easily prorated between business and personal use. In determining business mileage, consideration should be given to the following items:

Total mileage driven can often be ascertained from bills for repairs, oil changes, etc., near the beginning and end of the year since the bills frequently reflect mileage readings.

Assistance in the allocation of automobile expenses between business and personal use can sometimes be made by reference to the automobile insurance policy which usually states whether other members of the family operate the vehicles.

A review of gas and oil tickets may reveal signatures of the wife or children. This, of course, indicates personal use.

The total cost of gas for the year can also be used to estimate total mileage.

## Adequate Records

Records for substantiation of travel away from home, entertainment and business gift expenditures should be maintained in an account book, diary, statement of expense or similar record (supported by adequate documentary evidence) which is sufficient to establish the aforementioned elements of these expenditures.

The taxpayer is not required to record information in his/her account book, diary, or other record which would duplicate information reflected on a receipt of his/her account book or other record. He/she is not required to record in his/her account book or expense account record amounts an employer pays directly for any ticket or other travel item. However, if the taxpayer charges such items to his/her employer through a credit card or otherwise, he/she must make a record of such expenditures.

The account book, diary, statement of expense, or similar record should be prepared or maintained in such manner that the recording of the elements of an expenditure is made at or near the time the expenditure is made.

An expense account statement which is a transcription of an account book, diary, or similar record prepared or maintained in accordance with the rules set forth in the regulations shall be considered an adequate record of such expenses, provided the taxpayer submitted it to an employer or client or customer in the regular course of good business practice.

## Daily Diary

The reliance to be given the daily diary is one of the tax auditor's most common and recurring problems. The auditor must remember that the diary is just one type of required record to substantiate expense deductions. He/she does not have to accept the diary as being correct even though it conforms with the recordkeeping requirements of the regulations.

If the amount of expenses claimed in the diary is disproportionate when compared with the business activities and income of the taxpayer, or if the auditor has reasonable grounds for questioning the credibility of the taxpayer's entries, the taxpayer should be requested to submit further substantiation.

The auditor's experience based on audits of similar taxpayers will be of considerable help in determining whether to make the above request.

One method of determining the accuracy of daily entries when they appear excessive is to prepare an application of funds analysis. In other words, the total of all funds received from salaries, commission, drawings on account, investments, and savings accounts, less estimated amounts spent for living expenses, deposits to savings accounts and investments will reflect the maximum amount that could have been spent for entertainment. The tax auditor must remember that no real purpose is achieved in spending several hours in preparing an application of funds analysis when the total expense deducted appears reasonable when compared with the taxpayer's income and the type of business or where it may best be reasonably determined by other means.

## Business Purpose

The taxpayer may be required to submit a written statement to corroborate other evidence that an expenditure was for a business purpose. However, the degree of substantiation will vary according to the facts and circumstances in each case. Where the business purpose of an expenditure is evident, a written explanation is not required.

If food and beverages are furnished to an individual under circumstances generally considered to be conducive to a business discussion, and it is evident that there is a business relationship between the taxpayer and the person entertained, a written explanation of business purpose is not required.

## Documentary Evidence

In addition to the above, documentary evidence, such as receipts, paid bills, or similar evidence sufficient to support an expenditure is required for:

1. Any expenditure for lodging while traveling away from home, and
2. Any other expenditure of $25 or more, except that where such evidence is not readily available for transportation charges it will not be required.

Documentary evidence will ordinarily be considered adequate to support an expenditure if it discloses the amount, date, place, and essential character of the expenditure.

1. A hotel receipt is sufficient to support expenditures for business travel if it contains the name and location of the hotel, the date or dates the taxpayer stayed there, and separate amounts for charges such as, lodging, meals, telephone, etc.
2. A restaurant receipt is sufficient to support an expenditure for a business meal if it contains the name and location of the restaurant, the date and amount of the expenditure, and charges made for items other than meals and beverages.

Generally, a check drawn to cash is not evidence of a business expenditure without other evidence showing that the funds were used for a certain business purpose.

## Substantial Compliance—General

Regulations section 1.274-5(c)(2)(v) provides authority for allowing deductions in those cases where the taxpayer has substantially complied with the adequate records provisions, but fails to establish a particular element of an expenditure.

The taxpayer should be permitted to establish such element by evidence which the tax auditor deems adequate. This involves an evaluation of the quality of the evidence and the exercise of judgment and discretion on the part of the examiner.

The term "substantial compliance" is not defined in the regulations and is a question of degree. It is an area where the auditor must exercise judgment depending on the facts and circumstances in each case. In exercising judgment, the tax auditor should consider such factors as the number and type of expenditures involved, the number of missing elements and the nature thereof, the documentation missing, the reason why the element was not substantiated in accordance with the adequate records requirements, and the availability of other information to substantiate the expenditure.

Where the taxpayer generally has good records, the lack of an occasional receipt or other element will not prevent the records from being adequate if the evidence leads to a reasonable conclusion that a valid business expense was incurred. Application of this rule may be warranted in the case of home entertainment where it is frequently difficult to obtain a "meaningful" receipt.

If the taxpayer establishes the elements of time, place, business purpose, and business relationship to persons entertained, but has difficulty establishing the actual cost of food and beverage, the tax auditor should apply the substantial compliance rule in allowing a deduction for the cost of the home entertainment.

## Other Sufficient Evidence

If a taxpayer fails to meet the adequate records and substantial compliance level of proof with respect to each element of an expenditure, he/she may still substantiate such element by other sufficient evidence corroborating his/her own statement. Under this provision the taxpayer must establish such element—

1. By his/her own written statement containing detailed information as to such element, and

2. By other corroborative evidence sufficient to establish such element. If it is description of a gift, or the cost, time, place or date of an expenditure, the corroborative evidence shall be direct evidence, such as a statement in writing or oral testimony of persons entertained. If the element is either the business relationship between the taxpayer and the persons entertained or the business purpose of an expenditure the corroborative evidence may be circumstantial evidence.

## Exemptions and Dependents—General

If there is no exemption claimed for a spouse, particularly where dependent children are enumerated, or even where an exemption is claimed, attention should be given the box checked under Filing Status of page 1 of Form 1040, as to whether a separate return is being filed by the spouse.

## Support Test

In nonmultiple support cases where the claimed dependent resides in the taxpayer's home, difficulty is encountered in determining support. The reason is that amounts spent for the dependent's general support such as food, clothing and lodging are not the type that can be substantiated by ordinary documentation. The auditor should take into consideration the total income of the taxpayer and the number of persons in the family unit.

Detailed information concerning total support is unnecessary where the taxpayer's statement that he/she furnished the entire support of the dependent is accepted. However, such statement will be accepted only when supported by information that the dependent had no income or other funds of his/her own, received no aid from agencies or other individuals, and was not the owner of the dwelling which he/she occupied.

There are certain items that are not considered in total support, and the presence of these would not of themselves preclude the taxpayer from having furnished the sole support of the dependent. These items will be discussed later.

## Partial Support

Where there is a strong indication that the taxpayer did furnish more than one-half of the dependent's total support and it is accepted or established that the dependent was not claimed by others who are believed or known to have also furnished support, the exemption will generally be allowed the taxpayer without a showing of total support. For example, where the divorced mother acknowledges that the money received from the taxpayer for the support of their son was more than one-half of his total support and that she did not claim his exemption, the taxpayer may be allowed the exemption without a showing of total support.

If there is a strong reason to believe the taxpayer may not have furnished more than one-half of the dependent's total support, it will generally be necessary that information be furnished to substantiate the claim. This is particularly so where a claimed dependent enters the Armed Forces. In determining who contributed more than one-half the total support, consideration must be given to the basic support items furnished by the military for clothing, quarters, food, and medical care, as well as pay and allowances.

These cost figures vary with the cost-of-living index as well as with the various Branches of the Armed Forces. Although rule-of-thumb costs have not been established in this handbook, this does not preclude inquiry to the appropriate military authorities at the local level to obtain current cost figures to facilitate the audit.

## Amount of Total Support

It is the responsibility of the taxpayer claiming the dependent to show the amount of total support. Therefore, if the dependent does not reside in the taxpayer's household, it will generally be necessary for the taxpayer to secure the information relating to support from the other household or households in which the dependent resided during the year.

The term "support" includes food, shelter, clothing, medical and dental care, education, entertainment, haircuts, personal hygiene, travel, etc. However, cost of support does not include value of personal services.

The amount of each expense item may be accepted without verification if reasonable. No guideline can be furnished here as to what is to be considered as reasonable since this is a matter of judgment in which consideration must be given to the number of members in the household, available funds, area or country in which the dependent resided, standard of living, etc.

If the reported household expenses and the direct expenses of the dependent, together with itemized deductions and a reasonable estimate of unrelated expenses exceed reported income and other funds, it is evident that the expenses have been overstated or available funds understated.

In the absence of any other acceptable means of allocation, the dependent's total support will include a pro rata portion of general household expenses based on the number of members in the household. Generally, temporary absence of one or more members, including the dependent, will not make a material change in the allocation.

## Expenses of Support

Food—This is an item which generally cannot be substantiated and judgment is required in considering whether the reported amount is reasonable. Factors which may give rise to an unequal apportionment of the expense include: dependent requires special diet and therefore more expensive foods by reason of a physical ailment; most of the meals are eaten elsewhere; absence from the household for various periods, etc.

Shelter—This will include rents paid or the fair rental value of the lodging. Knowledge as to the fair market value of property, its location, and annual real estate taxes, may be of assistance in determining reasonableness of the reported rental value.

Clothing—In determining reasonableness of amounts spent for clothing, consideration must be given to age and sex of the dependent.

Medical and dental care—This is an item which can ordinarily be substantiated but, as in the case of clothing, the expense must be shown to have been incurred and paid on behalf of the taxpayer except where there is an approximation of the expense incurred for the entire household. The tax auditor should be alert to the fact that if the exemption is not allowable, by reason of the fact that the support test has not been met, any medical expenses of the dependent claimed as a deduction must also be disallowed.

In determining the amount furnished by the dependent himself/herself, the age of the dependent should lead to a question as to whether or not social security benefits, welfare payments, relief, or incidental earnings of the dependent should also be considered.

The dependent's own available funds must be determined as to amount and how expended. The source and tax status of the money is immaterial. Unless the taxpayer can establish otherwise, the dependent's available funds will be considered as having been used for his/her own support. However, if those funds are in the form of wages, consideration must be given to the fact that generally the entire wage is not available for support by reason of various payroll deductions. The auditor may also encounter situations where all or part of the dependent's funds are not expended, but deposited on account. This will require documentation by passbooks, bank statements, etc.

In the absence of records, where husband and wife each received social security in a joint check, one-half of the amount of that check expended for items of support will be considered as having been furnished by each, even though their benefits included in the check may differ.

Certain benefits received for or by the dependent for his/her support must be considered as having been so used regardless of how expended. These include:

1. A public benefit payments based solely on need;
2. Support received under a court order or divorce decree. (Arrearage payments received for child support are not considered as support payments.)

If the dependent resided in the taxpayer's household, the difference between the total amount spent for the support and the amounts furnished by the dependent and others will generally be accepted as having been furnished by the taxpayer.

If the dependent resided outside of the taxpayer's household, the taxpayer may be required to establish his/her contribution toward support by receipts, canceled checks, or statements.

In the case of support being furnished under the terms of a court order or divorce decree, it may be necessary to review the original document and all amendments. Amount paid will be considered as having been paid equally for each individual as provided for in the instrument. If alimony and support payments are both provided in the instrument but the amount of support is not specified, the total amount is considered as alimony.

Voluntary contributions toward expenses of a household in which the taxpayer was not a member will, in the absence of records of contributions by others within that household, be considered as having been given equally to all members. If a member of the household is also contributing in above, his/her contribution will be first applied toward his/her own support and the excess, if any, in the absence of records, will be considered as having been contributed equally toward the support of the other members.

## Medical Expenses

The expense paid must be for the medical care of the taxpayer, spouse, or the dependent of the taxpayer. A person is a "dependent" for medical deduction purposes if he/she meets all criteria for establishing an exemption for a dependent with the exception of the gross income test.

The expenses are deductible only in the year paid, regardless of the method of accounting used by the taxpayer. Advance payments are not deductible; however, prior years' medical expenses paid in the current year are deductible. Expenses paid in the particular year must be reduced to the extent they were reimbursed in the year. Reimbursement for expenses paid in a prior year are to be included in gross income in the year received to the extent the expenses caused a decrease in taxes for the prior year.

Particular attention should be given to the possible duplication of expenses claimed and the acceptance of unreceipted bills in general. For example, a hospital will present a taxpayer with a bill for $115 for a confinement. Because the taxpayer has a Blue Cross policy that provides $75 for confinements, only $40 is paid the hospital. The taxpayer then has the $115 unreceipted bill and a $40 receipt. Only the latter is deductible.

Similar duplicate deductions are claimed when the taxpayer actually pays the medical bill in total and subsequently receives an insurance settlement of all or part of the expenditure made. Since the absence of hospitalization insurance premium expense does not preclude the possibility of reimbursement, it should be determined what insurance coverage, if any, the taxpayer has.

Problems also arise in connection with the audit of amounts claimed for drugs and prescriptions or paid to the family doctor. If amounts in this category appear to be unreasonable an attempt should be made to tie them in with specific illnesses. Hospital bills are usually broken down as to the various charges thereon. Pharmaceutical charges appearing on a hospital bill should be segregated. Care should be exercised in the analysis of medicines and prescriptions in order to prevent the inclusion of various nondeductible expenses.

There are certain other nonqualifying expenses, such as food substitutes, trips for a change in environment, improvement of morale or a general improvement in health, which the tax auditor should look for.

Hospitalization and health insurance premiums are allowable only as medical expenses. Premium paid on life insurance, accident policies, and insurance for protection against loss of life, earnings, limbs, eyes, etc., are not deductible. If a policy provides for both deductible and nondeductible benefits, only that portion attributable to the coverage for medical expenses is deductible, and the premium paid must be allocated. If any doubt exists as to the coverage, it may be necessary for the taxpayer to secure the necessary data from his/her employer or insurance company.

Local transportation expenses can usually be accepted without verification if the amount is nominal. Mileage relating to a greater transportation expense should be ascertained through an analysis of receipts as to frequency and distance of the trips. Statements from physicians as to the purpose of trips other than local are generally required.

## Contributions

Contributions claimed by individuals are divided into two classes: Those fully substantiated and those paid in cash and no substantiation is available. The fully substantiated payments should be checked against the List of Exempt Organizations when any names are in doubt.

In recent years charitable organizations soliciting funds from the public have made it a practice to issue receipts for donations. This is the case in door-to-door solicitations by volunteer workers, such as a neighbor or occupant of an apartment building who solicits funds from his/her neighbors or other residents of the building. Similarly, many churches have instituted envelope systems and render periodic statements to their parishioners of the amounts contributed. Substantial donations, such as to building funds, are frequently made on a pledge basis and some record of payments is maintained by the church.

When auditing unsubstantiated cash contributions, the auditor should ask himself/herself this question: Is the total amount of contributions claimed reasonable in relation to the amount available out of which contributions could have been made? Such available cash must take into consideration the amount of gross income less the other deductions claimed on the return, personal living expenses, income taxes withheld and any estimated tax payments.

Once the tax auditor has considered the availability of cash, he/she should also look to the following: the care the taxpayer used in preparing the return, the amount of documentation which was offered for other items on the return; the preciseness with which he/she claimed other contributions; the practices of the church to which he/she belongs, and the number of children in the family.

In many churches, the practice of tithing is followed, i.e., the contribution of a certain percentage of income is made to the church. Where checks are not available for these amounts, a letter from the church or other satisfactory evidence should be sufficient to support the deduction.

Whether an item qualifies as a contribution is a factual matter. The taxpayer should be questioned concerning the nature and purpose of certain donations, such as contributions made to individuals. These are not deductible unless it is conclusively established that the individual is, in fact, a conduit through which the contribution is made to a qualified organization.

Amounts paid for such items as benefit performances, merchandise, goods, etc., the proceeds of which go exclusively to a charitable organization, would be deductible only to the extent they exceed the regular price or value of such items.

Where a taxpayer claims out-of-pocket expenses for transportation and meals and lodging while away from home overnight in rendering donated services to a qualified organization, the auditor should determine whether there was reimbursement by the organization. Nonreimbursed expense for the use of an automobile may be deducted at a standard mileage rate of 9¢ per mile or as actual expenses, such as gas, oil, etc. However, no deduction will be allowed for depreciation, insurance, or proportionate share of general maintenance or general repairs. Only those expenditures incurred for operation, maintenance, and repair which are directly attributable to the use of the automobile in performing gratuitous services for the organization are deductible. Expenses incurred to attend a church convention solely as a member of the church rather than as a duly chosen representative are not deductible.

Contributions to schools or to religious and educational organizations which sponsor schools, such as college alumni funds, which the taxpayer's dependents attend should be analyzed in order to determine whether part of the deduction claimed actually represents cost of tuition. Consideration also should be given to whether a tuition payment was discounted by all or part of the amount of the contribution. A statement secured by the taxpayer from the charitable organization explaining the purpose and amount of the contribution would facilitate the audit of this term.

In a case where property is contributed, verify the fair market value of the property at the time of gift and determine whether the donor retains any control over the property.

The taxpayer is responsible for furnishing the necessary evidence to establish the fair market value of donated property. Sentimental value to the contributor is not includible. Likewise, the value of the taxpayer's services is nondeductible. The original or replacement cost is not a correct measure of the fair market value. Self-serving statements of taxpayers are generally inconclusive. Often the information requires amplification to establish the true facts concerning the articles contributed. Statements by taxpayers and the charitable organization should be in as much detail as possible. If the charitable organization has no record of the sale of the articles contributed by the taxpayer, it may be able to advise concerning the average selling price of similar donated property. A general statement from a charitable organization showing a total estimated amount for articles contributed by a taxpayer without a breakdown of the value of each article is inconclusive.

In some situations, the circumstances under which the articles were donated and the use being made of the articles just prior to the time they were donated may be indicative of their general condition and value. Such donations are sometimes made incident to moving to avoid moving costs or when new furniture is purchased. In some instances where the cost and date of purchase is determinable, an approximate value of used furniture and similar articles can be determined by depreciating the cost based on the probable useful life. Any amounts allowed in the absence of conclusive evidence of the fair market value should be held to the minimum.

Where property is allegedly donated, such as an art object, but the taxpayer retains possession, the auditor should be certain a contribution has, in fact, been made.

## Educational Expense

The auditor should be familiar with the regulations, rulings, and decisions relating to this issue. A determination must be made as to the primary purpose of the educational course. If the taxpayer can show that he/she has met the minimum requirements of his/her position and that he/she is required to incur educational expenses to retain his/her salary, status, or employment, no relationship between the studies and the position need be established. For example, if an English teacher, holding a permanent teaching certificate, pursues studies in engineering and the six credits received from such studies meet the requirements to retain salary, status, or employment, the educational expenses incurred would be deductible.

However, if the taxpayer voluntarily incurs an educational expense, he/she must show that he/she has met the minimum requirements of the position and that the education was taken primarily to maintain or improve skills in that position. In addition to a transcript of studies, a statement from the employer as to past, present, and anticipated duties of the taxpayer and whether he/she has met the minimum requirements of the present or anticipated position may be necessary. If the studies do not bear a direct relationship to present duties, no deduction would be allowable. For example, no deduction would be allowable to a chemist pursuing studies in law, nor to a salesman taking a course in management in anticipation of promotion to sales manager.

The degree and type of teaching certificate held by a school teacher must be ascertained. If a teacher meets the minimum requirements of the local school board but not those of the State Board of Education, the educational expenses incurred in meeting the State's requirements are not deductible. If the minimum requirements of the local board exceed those of the State, a deduction is not allowable for educational expenses incurred in meeting the requirements of the local board.

A situation not uncommonly encountered is where an individual while attending a university takes work leading to a degree with the university providing employment (such as an instructor or research assistant). In such cases, the true picture must be determined—how, why, and when the taxpayer secured the employment. If the employment was secured at or near the time of attendance and studies and for the purpose of providing funds to pursue studies, it can hardly be said that the educational expenses were primarily incurred to increase proficiency in the taxpayer's present employment.

The taxpayer must not only establish the allowability of

the deduction but also establish the amount of the deduction. Receipts or other substantiation are required for cost of tuition, books, and similar expenses. Transportation and lodging expenses must also be substantiated. Auto mileage incurred in obtaining the education must be established. The Standard Mileage Rates may be used in determining the transportation costs.

If the educational expense involves overseas travel, the tour folio, registration receipt, and transcript of studies from the overseas educational institution may indicate the primary purpose of the travel. Consideration must be given to the amount of time devoted to personal activities as compared with the time devoted to educational pursuits. For example, if a taxpayer took an 8-week summer tour of South America and was enrolled and attended an accredited university for 2 weeks during this period, it is not likely that the primary purpose of the trip was to attend the university. Therefore the cost of transportation for the tour, as well as meals and lodging while not in attendance at the university would not be deductible. If the studies taken during this 2-week period were to improve the taxpayer's skills in his/her present position in which he/she has met the minimum requirements, the expense of tuition, books and other similar expenses, together with cost of meals and lodging during the 2-week period would be deductible. If the period of each activity were reversed, that is, 6 weeks of study and 2 weeks of sightseeing, the cost of transportation to and from South America together with expense of meals and lodging enroute and during the 6-week period at the university would be deductible. Of course, if the taxpayer did not pursue studies relating to his/her present position or had not met the minimum requirements of his/her position, none of the expenses during the 8-week period would be deductible.

## Alimony and Separate Maintenance

Usually amounts paid for alimony can be verified from canceled checks or other evidence of payment. If the payments are for support, under a decree of a domestic relations court, they can sometimes be verified from statements rendered by the court to the taxpayer since in some localities it is the practice of this court to collect and transmit the payments.

In any event, the agreement under which payments are made, such as court decree and amendments thereto, written separation agreement, or decree of support should be analyzed because of terms and dates that are material in determining deductibility under the Code. Payments for a combination of alimony and child support should be carefully analyzed especially when they constitute arrearages. If the payment does not equal the total obligation for segregated alimony and child support, the payment must first be applied to the child support obligation. Each periodic payment and obligation must be considered on a periodic rather than a calendar year basis. If the total payments for the year exceed the obligations for the particular year, the excess will be considered as payment of child support arrearages of prior years unless the taxpayer can establish that the excess exceeded such arrearages. Payments made on arrearages in alimony are deductible in the year paid.

Insurance premiums are considered as alimony paid to the wife if the policy has been irrevocably assigned to her, there being no chance that the husband or his estate will recapture the proceeds.

Payments on a home mortgage, as well as interest and real estate taxes, are not alimony payments if the husband has retained an interest of ownership in the property. The payments in part, however, may constitute an allowable deduction as interest and taxes.

The use of the husband's home by the divorced wife does not constitute a periodic payment and, therefore, is not an allowable deduction.

Counsel fees incurred by the husband are not deductible. Such fees paid by the husband for the wife are not periodic payments and are, therefore, not deductible.